ACTIVITY WORKBOOK

SIDE by SIDE

Plus

Steven J. Molinsky • Bill Bliss

with

Carolyn Graham • Peter S. Bliss

Contributing Authors

Dorothy Lynde • Elizabeth Handley

Illustrated by

Richard E. Hill

D1291907

ZB
May /2021

TO THE TEACHER

Side by Side Plus Activity Workbook 2 provides supplemental activities to accompany *Side by Side Plus Student Book 2*. The all-skills activities include listening comprehension practice, GrammarRaps, and GrammarSongs featured on the included Digital Audio CDs. New material in this edition includes activities to support the Student Book Gazette lessons and a new workbook section offering focused practice with lifeskill competencies and employment topics. An integrated numeracy curriculum provides practice with numbers, basic math, and word problems. A complete Answer Key enables students to use the Workbook independently for self-study.

(*Side by Side Plus Test Prep Workbook 2*, available separately, offers test preparation practice through achievement tests for all units of the program. The tests are also available as reproducibles included with *Side by Side Plus Teacher's Guide 2*.)

Side by Side Plus Activity Workbook 2

Pearson Education, 10 Bank Street, White Plains, NY 10606

Staff credits: The people who make up the *Side by Side Plus* team, representing content creation, design, manufacturing, marketing, multimedia, project management, publishing, rights management, and testing are Pietro Alongi, Allen Ascher, Rhea Banker, Elizabeth Barker, Lisa Bayrasli, Elizabeth Carlson, Jennifer Castro, Tracey Munz Cataldo, Diane Cipollone, Aerin Csigay, Victoria Denkus, Dave Dickey, Daniel Dwyer, Wanda España, Oliva Fernandez, Warren Fischbach, Pam Fishman, Nancy Flaggman, Patrice Fraccio, Irene Frankel, Aliza Greenblatt, Lester Holmes, Janet Johnston, Caroline Kasterine, Barry Katzen, Ray Keating, Renee Langan, Jaime Lieber, José Antonio Méndez, Julie Molnar, Pamela Pia, Stuart Radcliffe, Jennifer Raspiller, Kriston Reinmuth, Mary Perrotta Rich, Tania Saiz-Sousa, Katherine Sullivan, Paula Van Ells, Kenneth Volcjak, Paula Williams, and Wendy Wolf.

Text composition: TSI Graphics, Inc.
Illustrations: Richard E. Hill

The authors gratefully acknowledge the contribution of Tina Carver in the development of the original *Side by Side* program.

ISBN-10: 0-13-418680-X
ISBN-13: 978-0-13-418680-1

Printed in the United States of America

6 2020

Contents

A WHAT DO THEY LIKE TO DO?

| chat online | go hiking | go to the mall | play soccer | write letters |
| go dancing | go to the beach | listen to music | watch TV | |

1. He ___likes to___ ___watch TV___.

2. They _like to_ _play soccer_.

3. She _likes to_ _write letters_

4. I _like to_ _listen to music_.

5. They _like to_ _go dancing_.

6. He _likes to_ _chat online_.

7. She _likes to_ _go hiking_

8. We _like to_ _go to the mall_.

9. My dog _likes to_ _go to the beach_

B LISTENING

Listen and choose the correct response.

1. a. He likes to chat online.
   b. They like to chat online.

2. a. I like to dance.
   b. She likes to dance.

3. a. He likes to read.
   b. She likes to read.

4. a. They like to play basketball.
   b. We like to play basketball.

5. a. He likes to go to the library.
   b. We like to go to the library.

6. a. You like to go to the mall.
   b. I like to go to the mall.

7. a. We like to play loud music.
   b. He likes to play loud music.

8. a. She likes to watch TV.
   b. They like to watch TV.

WHAT DO THEY LIKE TO DO?

bake	go	listen	ride	sing	watch

1. Alan likes to _____ watch _____ TV.

   _____ He watches _____ TV every day.

   _____ He watched _____ TV yesterday.

   _____ He's going to watch _____ TV
   tomorrow.

2. I like to _____ listen to _____ to music.

   I listen _____ to music every day.

   I listened _____ to music yesterday.

   I am going to listen _____ to music
   tomorrow.

3. Thelma likes to _____ ride _____ her bicycle.

   She rides _____ her bicycle every day.

   She rode _____ her bicycle yesterday.

   She's going to ride her bicycle
   tomorrow.

4. My parents like to sing together.

   They sing together _____ every day.

   They sang together _____ yesterday.

   They're going to sing together
   tomorrow.

5. My wife and I like to _____ bake _____ cookies.

   We bake _____ cookies every day.

   We baked _____ cookies yesterday.

   We're going to bake _____ cookies
   tomorrow.

6. Brian likes to _____ go _____ sailing.

   He goes _____ sailing every day.

   He went _____ sailing yesterday.

   He's going to go _____ sailing
   tomorrow.

D LIKES AND DISLIKES

| clean | cook | drive | eat | feed | go | read | take | wait | watch |

| like to
likes to | don't like to
doesn't like to |

1. Ronald ___likes to cook___ spaghetti.

2. Sally ___doesn't like to take___ the subway.

3. My children _like to feed_ the birds in the park.

4. Ted and Amy _don't like to eat_ in noisy restaurants.

5. My wife _likes to read_ novels.

6. Arnold _doesn't like to wait_ for the bus.

7. My friends and I _like to watch_ videos.

8. I _don't like to drive_ downtown.

9. Howard _likes to clean_ his house.

10. Tim and Jim _don't like to go_ to the doctor.

E WRITE ABOUT YOURSELF

What do you like to do?

I like to _visit my native country_
I _like to travel around America_
I _like to cook vietnamese foods_
I _like to plant the flower_
I _like to learn English language_
and more

What don't you like to do?

I don't like to _hear noisy sounds_
I _don't like to go out in winter_
I _don't like to use air conditioner_
I _don't like get in traffic jam_
I _don't like go fishing_

F DAY AFTER DAY

do	get up	go	make	plant	play	study	visit	wash	write

1. Tim _____ _washes_ _____ his car every day.

_____ _He washed_ _____ his car yesterday.

_____ _He's going to wash_ _____ his car tomorrow.

2. Alice _wakes up_ early every morning.

She waked up early yesterday morning.

She's going to wake up early tomorrow morning.

3. Millie and Max _are_ dancing every Friday.

They went _____ dancing last Friday.

They're going to go _____ dancing next Friday.

4. I _learn_ _____ English every evening.

I learned _____ English yesterday evening.

I'm going to learn _____ English tomorrow evening.

(continued)

5. The man next door ___play___ the drums every night.

___He played___ the drums last night.

___He's going to play___ the drums tomorrow night.

6. My mother ___makes___ pancakes for breakfast every Sunday.

___She made___ pancakes last Sunday.

___She's going to make___ pancakes next Sunday.

7. My wife and I ___plant___ flowers every spring.

___We planted___ flowers last spring.

___We're going to plant___ flowers next spring.

8. Steven ___writes a letter___ to his girlfriend every week.

___He wrote a letter___ to her last week.

___He's going to write a letter___ to her next week.

9. Julie ___visits___ her grandparents every weekend.

___She visited___ them last weekend.

___She's going to visit___ them next weekend.

10. My husband and I ___do___ yoga every afternoon.

___We did___ yoga yesterday afternoon.

___We're going to do___ yoga tomorrow afternoon.

11. I ___like to go for walk___ every ___day___.

I ___went for walk yesterday___

I'm ___going to go for walk tomorrow___

GRAMMARRAP: *I Don't Like to Rush*

Listen. Then clap and practice.

I don't like to rush. Do you?
I don't like to hurry.
I don't like to get upset.
I don't like to worry.

I'm not going to rush. Are you?
I'm not going to hurry.
I'm not going to get upset.
I'm not going to worry!

H **GRAMMARRAP:** *He Doesn't Like to Watch TV*

Listen. Then clap and practice.

He doesn't like to watch TV.
He doesn't like to dance.
He doesn't like to cook or sew
or wash or iron his pants.

She doesn't like to go to the beach.
She doesn't like to shop.
She doesn't like to vacuum her rugs
or dust or wax or mop.

I WHAT'S PAULA GOING TO GIVE HER FAMILY?

cell phone
gloves
CD player
novel
dog
plant
watch
sweater

Paula is looking for presents for her family. Here's what she's going to give them.

1. Her husband's hands are always cold.   _____She's going to give him gloves._____

2. Her daughter loves animals.   _____

3. Her son never arrives on time.   _____

4. Her parents like to listen to music.   _____

5. Her sister likes clothes.   _____

6. Her brother likes to read.   _____

7. Her grandparents like flowers.   _____

8. Her cousin Charlie likes to talk to his friends.   _____

J PRESENTS

1. Last year I ___gave___ my husband pajamas.

   This year ___I'm going to give him___ a bathrobe.

2. Last year Bobby _____ his grandmother candy.

   This year _____ flowers.

3. Last year Carol _____ her boyfriend a tee shirt.

   This year _____ sweat pants.

4. Last year we _____ our children a bird.

   This year _____ a dog.

5. Last year I _____ my girlfriend perfume.

   This year _____ a ring.

6. Last year we _____ our son a sweater.

   This year _____ a bicycle.

7. Last year I ....

   This year ....

| he | her | him | I | me | she | they | them | us | we | you |

1. A. What did you give your wife for her birthday?

B. _____I_____ gave _____her_____ earrings.

2. A. What did your children give you for your birthday?

B. _____ gave _____ a book.

3. A. What did Michael give his parents for their anniversary?

B. _____ gave _____ a CD player.

4. A. What did your friends give you and your husband for your anniversary?

B. _____ gave _____ a plant.

5. A. What did your wife give you for your birthday?

B. _____ gave _____ a briefcase.

6. A. What did you and your wife give your son for his birthday?

B. _____ gave _____ a bicycle.

7. A. I forget. What did you give me for my last birthday?

B. _____ gave _____ a painting.

8. A. I forget. What did I give you for *your* last birthday?

B. _____ gave _____ a dress.

1st	first	7th	seventh	13th	thirteenth	19th	nineteenth	50th	fiftieth
2nd	second	8th	eighth	14th	fourteenth	20th	twentieth	60th	sixtieth
3rd	third	9th	ninth	15th	fifteenth	21st	twenty-first	70th	seventieth
4th	fourth	10th	tenth	16th	sixteenth	22nd	twenty-second	80th	eightieth
5th	fifth	11th	eleventh	17th	seventeenth	30th	thirtieth	90th	ninetieth
6th	sixth	12th	twelfth	18th	eighteenth	40th	fortieth	100th	one hundredth

L MATCHING

_b_	1.	eighth	**a.** 2nd	____	5.	thirty-third	**e.** 14th
____	2.	one hundredth	**b.** 8th	____	6.	thirteenth	**f.** 13th
____	3.	second	**c.** 20th	____	7.	fourteenth	**g.** 40th
____	4.	twentieth	**d.** 100th	____	8.	fortieth	**h.** 33rd

M WHAT'S THE NUMBER?

1. fiftieth   _50th_   6. first _____
2. ninety-ninth _____   7. sixteenth _____
3. fifteenth _____   8. sixty-fifth _____
4. twelfth _____   9. eighty-fourth _____
5. seventy-seventh _____   10. thirty-sixth _____

N LISTENING

Listen and write the ordinal number you hear.

1. barber shop   _2nd_
2. Wong family   _____
3. Acme Company   _____
4. Bob Richards   _13th_
5. bank   _3rd_
6. dentist's office   _9th_
7. flower shop   _1st_
8. Martinez family   _19th_
9. Louise Lane   _17th_
10. computer store   _first_

11. French restaurant   _38th_
12. my apartment   _8th_
13. Park family   _____
14. Dr. Jacobson   _6th_
15. Walker family   _2nd_
16. health club   _18th_

O RICHARD'S BIRTHDAYS

Fill in the missing words.

On Richard's 7th birthday, he (have) ___had___¹ a party at home. His mother (make) _____² pizza, and his father (bake) _____³ a cake. Richard's parents (give) _____⁴ him a new dog. Richard's friends (love) _____⁵ his birthday party because they (play) _____⁶ with his new dog, but Richard was upset because his mother didn't (give) _____⁷ the dog any cake to eat.

On Richard's 10th birthday, he (go) _____⁸ to the beach with his friends. They (swim) _____⁹ at the beach, and they (go) _____¹⁰ to a restaurant to eat. Richard's friends (like) _____¹¹ his birthday party, but Richard was upset because he didn't (like) _____¹² his present. His friends (give) _____¹³ him a wallet, but he (want) _____¹⁴ a baseball.

On Richard's 13th birthday, he (have) _____¹⁵ a picnic. His mother (cook) _____¹⁶ hot dogs and hamburgers. They (eat) _____¹⁷ delicious food and (play) _____¹⁸ baseball. All of his friends (enjoy) _____¹⁹ his birthday party, but Richard was upset because the girls didn't (talk) _____²⁰ to him.

On Richard's 16th birthday, he didn't (have) _____²¹ a party. He (go) _____²² dancing with his girlfriend, and he (have) _____²³ a wonderful time. His friends didn't (give) _____²⁴ him presents and his parents didn't (cook) _____²⁵. But Richard wasn't upset because he (dance) _____²⁶ with his girlfriend all night.

P MATCHING

__b__ 1. Richard didn't like his present _____.
__d__ 2. He went dancing _____.
__a__ 3. His parents gave him a dog _____.
__c__ 4. The girls didn't talk to Richard _____.

    a. on his 7th birthday
    b. on his 10th birthday
    c. on his 13th birthday
    d. on his 16th birthday

A WHAT'S THE FOOD?

apples	cheese	ice cream	meat	pepper	
bread	eggs	ketchup	mustard	potatoes	
cake	flour	lettuce	onions	soy sauce	
carrots	grapes	mayonnaise	oranges	tomatoes	

1. _tomatoes_

2. _carrots_

3. _grapes_

4. _potatoes_

5. _Ice cream_

6. _apples_

7. _lettuce_

8. _bread_

9. _cake_

10. _flour_

11. _onions_

12. _Ketchup_

13. _Majonare_

14. _eggs_

15. _meat_

16. _orange_

17. _Soy Sauce_

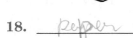

18. _pepper_

19. _Cheese_

20. _Mustard_

B WHAT ARE THEY SAYING?

Where's	Where are	It's	They're

1. A. _____Where's_____ the butter?

   B. _____It's_____ in the refrigerator.

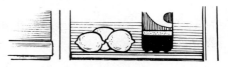

2. A. _____Where are_____ the bananas?

   B. _____They're_____ on the counter.

3. A. _____Where's_____ the salt?

   B. _____It's_____ in the cabinet.

4. A. _____Where_____ the lemons?

   B. _____They're_____ in the refrigerator.

5. A. _____Where're_____ the cookies?

   B. _____They're_____ in the cabinet.

6. A. _____Where's_____ the chicken?

   B. _____It's_____ in the freezer.

7. A. _____Where're_____ the pears?

   B. _____They're_____ on the counter.

8. A. _____Where's_____ the rice?

   B. _____It's_____ in the cabinet.

C LISTENING

Listen and choose the correct response.

1. (a.) It's on the counter.
   b. They're on the counter.

2. a. It's in the refrigerator.
   (b.) They're in the refrigerator.

3. (a.) It's in the freezer.
   b. They're in the freezer.

4. a. It's in the cabinet.
   (b.) They're in the cabinet.

5. (a.) It's on the counter.
   b. They're on the counter.

6. (a.) It's in the cabinet.
   (b.) They're in the cabinet.

7. a. It's on the counter.
   (b.) They're on the counter.

8. (a.) It's in the refrigerator.
   b. They're in the refrigerator.

Look at the menu to see what Randy's Restaurant has and doesn't have today.

Today's Menu
spaghetti
hamburgers
salad
ice cream
apple pie
milk
soda

1. A. May I have a hamburger and some french fries?

   B. I'm sorry, but _____*there aren't*_____

   _____*any french fries*_____.

2. A. May I please have a salad and some tea?

   B. I'm sorry, but _____*there isn't*_____

   _____*any tea*_____.

3. A. May I have chicken and some milk?

   B. I'm sorry, but *there aren't*

   any chicken and some milk.

4. A. May I have ice cream and some cookies?

   B. I'm sorry, but *there isn't*

   any ice cream.

5. A. May I have cake and some soda?

   B. I'm sorry, but *There aren't*

   any cake and some soda.

6. A. May we have two sandwiches, please?

   B. I'm sorry, but *there aren't*

   any sandwiches.

7. A. May I have apple pie and some orange juice?

   B. I'm sorry, but _____

   _____.

8. A. May I have spaghetti and some meatballs?

   B. I'm sorry, but _____

   _____.

THERE ISN'T/THERE AREN'T

1. There _____isn't any mayonnaise_____.

   How about some _____mustard_____?

2. There _____aren't any bananas_____.

   How about some _____grapes_____?

3. There _____isn't any meat_____.

   How about some _____fish_____?

4. There _____aren't any apple_____.

   How about some _____pears_____?

5. There _____isn't any ice cream_____.

   How about some _____yogurt_____?

6. There _____aren't any potatoes_____.

   How about some _____rice ?_____?

7. There _____isn't any tomatoes_____.

   How about some _____onions_____?

8. There _____isn't any milk_____.

   How about some _____orange juice_____?

LISTENING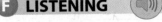

Listen and put a check (✓) under the correct picture.

1. _____ ✔

2. _____ ✓

3. _____ ✓

4. _____ ✓

5. _____ ✓

6. _____ ✓

G WHAT'S THE WORD?

how much	too much	how many	too many	a little	a few

1. A. _____How many_____ meatballs do you want?

   B. Not _____too many_____.

   Just _____a few_____.

2. A. _____How much_____ cheese do you want?

   B. Not _____too much_____.

   Just _____a little_____.

3. A. _____ ice cream do you want?

   B. Not _____too much_____.

   Just _____little_____.

4. A. _____How many_____ cookies do you want?

   B. Not _____too many_____.

   Just _____a few_____.

5. A. _____How much_____ lemonade do you want?

   B. Not _____too much_____.

   Just _____a little_____.

6. A. _____How many_____ oranges do you want?

   B. Not _____too many_____.

   Just _____a few_____.

H WHAT'S THE PROBLEM?

too much	too many

1. She cooked _____too many_____ meatballs.

2. He drinks _____too much_____ soda.

3. They ate _____too much_____ ice cream.

4. Henry had _____too many_____ onions.

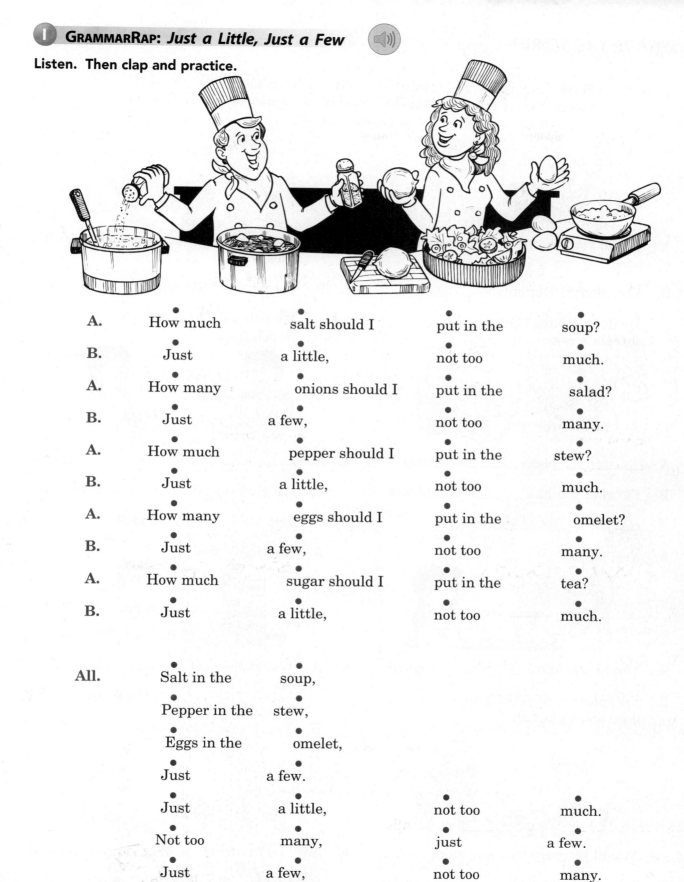

A.	How much	salt should I	put in the	soup?
B.	Just	a little,	not too	much.
A.	How many	onions should I	put in the	salad?
B.	Just	a few,	not too	many.
A.	How much	pepper should I	put in the	stew?
B.	Just	a little,	not too	much.
A.	How many	eggs should I	put in the	omelet?
B.	Just	a few,	not too	many.
A.	How much	sugar should I	put in the	tea?
B.	Just	a little,	not too	much.

All. Salt in the soup,

Pepper in the stew,

Eggs in the omelet,

Just a few.

Just a little, not too much.

Not too many, just a few.

Just a few, not too many.

Not too many, just one or two.

little	much	this	is	it's	it
few	many	these	are	they're	them

1. A. Would you care for some more chocolate cake?

   B. Yes, please. But only a ___little___.

   My dentist says I eat too ___much___ chocolate cake.

2. A. Would you care for some more french fries?

   B. Yes, please. But only a ___few___.

   My wife says I eat too ___many___ french fries.

3. A. ___I like___ pizza ___It's___ fantastic.

   B. I'm glad you like ___it___. Would you care for a ___little___ more?

   A. Yes, please.

4. A. ___I like___ potatoes ___They're___ good.

   B. I'm glad you like ___them___. Would you care for a ___few___ more?

   A. No, thank you.

5. A. Would you like a ___little___ yogurt?

   B. Yes, please. My doctor says ___it's___ good for my health.

6. A. Would you care for some cookies? I baked ___them___ this morning.

   B. Yes, please. But just a ___few___.

7. A. Would you care for some more pie?

   B. Yes, please. I know _____ bad for my health, but I really like _____.

8. A. You're eating too ___many___ meatballs!

   B. I know. But ___they're___ really good. Can I have just a ___few___ more?

K MATCHING

_e_ 1. This pie is very good!

_j_ 2. How do you like the hamburgers?

_h_ 3. I think these cookies are excellent!

_c_ 4. How much rice do you want?

_i_ 5. Where's the tea?

_g_ 6. Let's make some lemonade!

_b_ 7. How do you like the pizza?

_d_ 8. Where are the bananas?

_f_ 9. How many carrots do you want?

_a_ 10. Let's bake a cake for dessert!

a. We can't. There isn't any flour.

b. I think it's delicious.

c. Just a little.

d. They're on the counter.

e. I'm glad you like it.

f. Just a few.

g. We can't. There aren't any lemons.

h. I'm glad you like them.

i. It's in the cabinet.

j. I think they're delicious.

L LISTENING

Listen and put a check (✓) under the correct picture.

1.
  _____
 ✓

2.
 ✓
 _____

3.
 ✓ _____
 _____

4.
 _____
 ✓

5.
 _____
 ✓

6.
 ✓
 _____

7.
 ✓
 _____

8.
 _____
 ✓

9.
 _____
 ✓

10.
 ✓
 _____

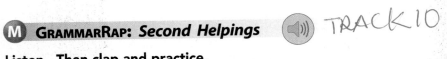
Listen. Then clap and practice.

All.   Not too   much, just   a little,
         Not too   many, just   a few.
         Not too   much, just   a little,
         Not too   many, just   a few.

A.   Would you   like more   chicken?
B.   Just   a little.
A.   Would you   like more   carrots?
B.   Just   a few.
A.   Would you   like more   gravy?
B.   Just   a little.
A.   Would you   like more   mushrooms?
B.   Just   a few.
A.   Would you   like more   salad?
B.   Just   a little.
A.   Would you   like more   tomatoes?
B.   Just   a few.
A.   Would you   like more   coffee?
B.   Just   a little.
A.   Would you   like more   cookies?
B.   Just   a few.

All.   Not too   much, just   a little.
         Not too   many, just   a few.
         Not too   much, just   a little.
         Not too   many, just   a few.

STUDENT BOOK
PAGES **19–26**

bag	bunch	can	gallon	jar	loaf/loaves
bottle	box	dozen	head	pound	of

1. Jack is going to buy food at the supermarket.

Jack's Shopping List

a ___can___ ___of___ soup
a ___head___ ___of___ lettuce
a ___bottle___ ___of___ ketchup
a ___pound___ ___of___ cheese
a ___bag___ ___of___ flour

2. Jennifer is going to make breakfast for her parents.

Jennifer's Shopping List

a ___box___ ___of___ cereal
a ___jar___ ___of___ jam
a ___loaf___ ___of___ bread
a ___bunch___ ___of___ bananas
a ___dozen___ ___ eggs

3. Mr. and Mrs. Baxter are going to have a birthday party for their daughter.

The Baxters' Shopping List

3 _____ _____ ice cream
2 ___box___ ___of___ cookies
2 ___pound___ ___of___ grapes
3 ___pound___ ___of___ meat
2 ___bag___ ___of___ bread

4. What are YOU going to buy this week?

Your Shopping List

2 bunch of bananas
1 head of lettuce
1 whole chicken
2 loy of bread
1 dole of eggs

B WHAT ARE THEY SAYING?

bananas	cheese	cookies	ice cream	jam	onions

1. Do we need anything from the supermarket?

   Do we need anything else?

   Yes. We need a jar of _____jam_____.

   Yes. We need a pint of _____Ice cream_____.

2. What do we need from the supermarket?

   Do we need anything else?

   We need a bunch of _____.

   Yes. We need a box of _____.

3. Do we need anything from the supermarket?

   Do we need anything else?

   Yes. We need a bag of _____.

   Yes. We need a half a pound of _____.

C LISTENING 🔊

Listen to the conversations. Put a check (✓) under the foods you hear.

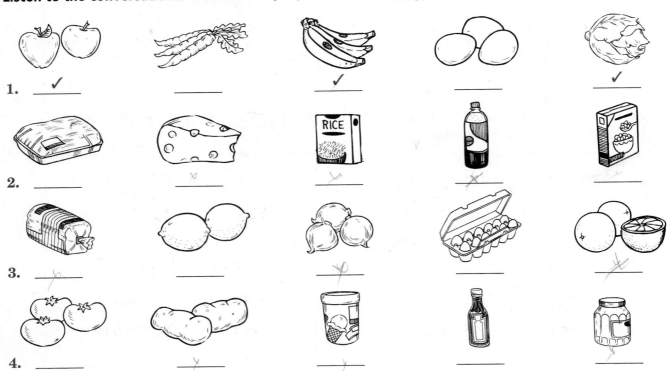

1. ___✓___   _____   ___✓___   _____   ___✓___

2. _____   _____   _____   _____   _____

3. _____   _____   _____   _____   _____

4. _____   _____   _____   _____   _____

Listen. Then clap and practice.

All.   We need   bread.

Whole wheat bread.

A.   How many   loaves do we need?

All.   Two.

All.   We need   beans.

Black   beans.

B.   How many   cans do we need?

All.   Three.

All.   We need   rice.

Brown   rice.

C.   How many   pounds do we need?

All.   Four.

All.   We need   jam.

Strawberry   jam.

D.   How many   jars do we need?

All.   Five.

All.   We need   milk.

Fresh   milk.

E.   How many   quarts do we need?

All.   Six.

All.   We need   cash.

We need   money.

F.   How much   money do we need?

All.   A lot!

are	cost	does	loaf	money	of	quart
bread	costs	is	loaves	much	pound	right

1. A. How ___much___ does a ___quart___ of milk ___cost___ ?

   B. A ___quart___ of ___milk___ ___costs___ two thirty-nine.

   A. Two dollars and thirty-nine cents?! That's a lot of ___money___ !

   B. You're ___right___ . Milk ___is___ very expensive this week.

2. A. How ___much___ does a ___loaf___ ___of___ bread cost?

   B. A ___loaf___ of ___bread___ ___costs___ one twenty-nine.

   A. Good! I'll take six ___loaves___ , please.

   B. Six ___loaves___ ?! That's a lot ___of___ bread!

   A. I know. But ___bread___ ___is___ very cheap this week!

3. A. How ___much___ ___does___ a ___pound___ of apples cost?

   B. A ___pound___ ___of___ apples ___costs___ three sixty-five.

   A. Three sixty five?! That's too ___much___ money!

   B. You're right. Apples ___are___ very expensive today,

   but bananas ___are___ very cheap.

   A. That's nice. But how can I make an apple pie with bananas?!

Listen and circle the price you hear.

1. $1.95   ($1.99)   4. $25   (25¢)   7. ($3.13) $3.30

2. ($5)   5¢   5. $2.74   ($2.47)   8. $1.15   ($1.50)

3. ($4.79) $9.47   6. ($6.60)   ($6.16) 9. ($2.10) $21

hot coffe : A hear break

WHAT'S THE WORD?

1. A. What would you like for breakfast?
   B. Please give me an order of _____.
      a. cereal
      (b.) scrambled eggs

2. A. What would you like to drink?
   B. I want a glass of _milk_
      (a.) milk
      b. coffee

3. A. What would you like for lunch?
   B. I want a bowl of _soup_
      a. pancakes
      (b.) soup

4. A. Would you care for some dessert?
   B. Yes. I'd like a dish of _ice cream_
      (a.) ice cream
      b. hot chocolate

5. A. What would you like?
   B. Please give me a cup of _tea_.
      (a.) tea
      b. cake

6. A. What would you like for dessert?
   B. I'd like a piece of _apple pie_
      a. strawberries
      (b.) apple pie

H **WHERE WOULD YOU LIKE TO GO FOR LUNCH?**

are	glass	many	order
bowl	is	much	piece
cup	it	of	they
dish			

A. Where would you like to go for lunch?

B. Let's go to Carla's Cafe. Their spaghetti ___is___¹ out of this world and ___it___² isn't expensive. I had an ___order___³ ___of___⁴ spaghetti there last week for a dollar ninety-five.

A. I don't really want to go to Carla's Cafe. Their spaghetti ___is___⁵ very good, but you can't get any chocolate milk. I like to have a ___cup___⁶ of chocolate milk with my lunch.

B. How about The Pancake Place? Their pancakes ___are___⁷ fantastic, and ___they___⁸ aren't expensive. An ___order___⁹ ___of___¹⁰ pancakes costs two sixty-nine.

A. I really don't like The Pancake Place. The pancakes ___are___¹¹ tasty, but their salad ___is___¹² terrible! It has too ___much___¹³ lettuce and too ___many___¹⁴ onions.

B. Well, how about Rita's Restaurant? Their desserts are wonderful. You can get a delicious ___of___¹⁵ _apple_¹⁶ pie, a ___bowl___¹⁷ ___of___¹⁸ strawberries, or a ___glass___¹⁹ ___of___²⁰ ice cream.

A. I know. But their hot chocolate ___is___²¹ very bad. I like to have a ___cup___²² ___of___²³ hot chocolate with my dessert.

B. Wait a minute! I know where we can go for lunch. Let's go to YOUR house!

I GRAMMARRAP: *Grocery List*  track 14

Listen. Then clap and practice.

We need a loaf of   bread
And a jar of   jam,
A box of   cookies
And a pound of   ham.
A bottle of   ketchup,
A pound of   cheese,
A dozen   eggs,
And a can of   peas.
A head of   lettuce,
Half a pound of   rice,
A bunch of   bananas,
And a bag of   ice.

a loaf of bread
a jar of jam
a box of cookies
a pound of ham
a bottle of ketchup

J GRAMMARRAP: *What Would You Like to Have?*

Listen. Then clap and practice.

A.   What would you like to   order?
     What would you like to   have?

B.   An order of   chicken,   a dish of   potatoes,
     A large green   salad   with a lot of   tomatoes.
     A bowl of   soup,   an order of   rice,
     And a glass of   soda   with a lot of   ice.

A.   And what would you like for   dessert?

B.   Nothing,   thanks.   I'm not very   hungry!

An order of

K WHAT'S THE WORD?

1. Slice the honey / (carrots).

2. Cut up the oranges / salt.

3. Chop up the flour / nuts.

4. Pour in the (water) / potatoes.

5. Slice the baking soda / (apples).

6. Pour it into the mixing (bowl) / recipe.

7. (Mix in) / Put the raisins.

8. Add / (Cook) for two hours.

L WHAT'S THE RECIPE?

a little   a few

Millie's Tomato Sauce

1. Put ____a little____ butter into a pan.

2. Chop up ____a few____ onions.

3. Cut up ____a few____ mushrooms and ____a little____ cheese.

4. Slice ____a few____ tomatoes.

5. Add ____a little____ salt and ____a little____ pepper.

6. Cook for _____ minutes.

M LISTENING

Listen and choose the correct word to complete the sentence.

1. a. onions
   (b.) water

2. a. cheese
   (b.) nuts

3. (a.) oranges
   b. baking soda

4. (a.) salt
   b. raisins

5. a. tomato
   (b.) potatoes

6. (a.) pepper
   b. mushrooms

Activity Workbook   **27**

A. Fill in the blanks.

Ex. a _____quart_____
of milk

1. a ___bunch___
of bananas

2. a ___can___
of soup

3. a ___bag___
of onions

4. a ___piece___
of pie

5. 2 ___box___
of cereal

6. 2 ___loaves___
of bread

B. Circle the correct answers.

Ex. Yogurt (is) / are cheap today.

1. I eat too much / (many) cookies.

2. She ate so (much) / many cake that

she has a stomachache.

3. What do you like / (like to) do on the

weekend?

4. How (much) / many does a bowl of

strawberries cost?

5. Would you care for a (little) / few grapes?

I bought (it) / them this morning, and

(it's) / they're very fresh.

6. (This) / These rice (is) / are delicious. May I

have a (little) / few more?

C. Complete the sentences.

Ex. Janet watches TV every Friday.

___She watched___ TV last Friday.

___She's going to watch___ TV next Friday.

1. Alan drives to the mall every week.

He ___drove___ to the mall last week.

___He's going to drive___
to the mall next week.

2. I go on vacation every year.

I ___went___ on vacation last year.

___I'm going to go___
on vacation next year.

3. We play baseball every Saturday.

We _played_ baseball last Saturday.

we're going to play
baseball next Saturday.

4. My sister writes letters to her friends every weekend.

She _wrote_ letters to her friends last weekend.

She's going to write
letters to her friends next weekend.

5. Ed makes pancakes every morning.

He _made_ pancakes yesterday morning.

He's going to make
pancakes tomorrow morning.

D.   Complete the sentences.

Ex. Last year my parents gave me a sweater for my birthday.

This year _they're going to give me_
a jacket.

1. Last year Tom gave his girlfriend flowers.

This year _Tom's going to_
give her candy.

2. Last year Sue gave her husband a CD player.

This year _Sue is going to_
give him a briefcase.

3. Last year we gave our parents a cell phone.

This year _I'm going to_
give them a computer.

E.   Listen and circle the correct word.

"I'm sorry, but there _____ any."

Ex. isn't / (aren't)

1. (isn't) / aren't

2. isn't / (aren't)

3. (isn't) / aren't

4. isn't / (aren't)

5. isn't / (aren't)

A FOOD SHOPPING

Read the article on student book page 27 and answer the questions.

1. In the past, people shopped _____.
   a. at supermarkets
   b. online
   c. at open markets
   d. at wholesale stores

2. Today people don't have to shop every day because _____.
   a. they have refrigerators
   b. they have busy lives
   c. many stores sell food at low prices
   d. it's difficult to keep food fresh

3. *Enormous* in paragraph 3 means very _____.
   a. cheap
   b. large
   c. modern
   d. busy

4. People shop at wholesale stores because _____.
   a. the stores deliver food to their homes
   b. the food is always very fresh
   c. they don't like large stores
   d. they want to save money

5. Open markets are always _____.
   a. outside
   b. in the city
   c. open 24 hours a day
   d. small

6. Today most people shop for food _____.
   a. almost every day
   b. on the Internet
   c. once or twice a week
   d. every day

7. *People still shop in little food stores* means _____.
   a. they like to shop in little food stores
   b. they can't shop in little food stores
   c. they rarely shop in little food stores
   d. they shopped in little food stores in the past, and they shop in them now

8. The main idea of this article is that _____.
   a. refrigerators keep food fresh
   b. people shop for food in different ways
   c. today's stores sell food at low prices
   d. it's convenient to shop on the Internet

B BUILD YOUR VOCABULARY! Crossword

Across

2.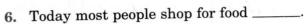

3.

4.

7.

8.

Down

1.

6.

5.

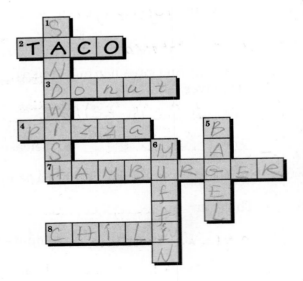

devil;

Look at the Fact File on student book page 27 and answer the questions.

1. Hens produce _____.
   a. rice
   b. cocoa
   c. eggs
   d. chocolate

2. According to the fact file, the world produces more than _____ eggs a day.
   a. 200,000,000,000
   b. 2,000,000,000 _ti? (2 billion)_
   c. 200,000,000
   d. 20,000,000

3. It takes 8,818 tons of cocoa beans to make _____ chocolate bars.
   a. 7,000,000
   b. 70,000,000
   c. 700,000,000 _million (triệu)_
   d. 7,000,000,000

4. The world produces _____ tons of rice a day.
   a. 1,000,006
   b. 1,000,600
   c. 1,000,060
   d. 1,600,000 _million tấn_

5. Cyprus is a very large _____.
   a. city
   b. pyramid
   c. island
   d. omelet

6. The world produces more than a million and a half _____ every day.
   a. tons of cocoa beans
   b. tons of rice
   c. tons of chocolate bars
   d. tons of cocoa bars

7. The world produces _____ pounds of cocoa beans every day. (There are 2,000 pounds in a ton.)
   a. 8,818
   b. 17,636
   c. 700,000,000
   d. 17,636,000

8. According to the Fact File, the world produces more than _____ in a week.
   a. 14 billion eggs
   b. 70,000 tons of cocoa
   c. 14 million tons of rice
   d. 7 billion chocolate bars

Match the "can do" statement and the correct sentence.

_e_ 1. I can tell about favorite activities.

_i_ 2. I can ask about past activities.

_a_ 3. I can ask about future plans.

_h_ 4. I can compliment about food. _bổ sung_

_b_ 5. I can express gratitude. _lòng biết ơn_

_j_ 6. I can get someone's attention.

_d_ 7. I can give instructions.

_g_ 8. I can ask for a recommendation.

_c_ 9. I can make a recommendation.

_f_ 10. I can agree with someone.

a. What are you going to do next weekend?

b. Thanks.

c. I suggest our chicken soup.

d. Chop up a few onions.

e. I like to go hiking.

f. You're right.

g. What do you recommend?

h. Your cake is delicious.

i. What did you do yesterday?

j. Excuse me.

1. A. Will you be back soon?

B. Yes, _____I will_____. _____I'll_____

_____be back_____ in half an hour.

2. A. Will the game begin soon?

B. Yes, _it will_. _it'll_

begin in ten minutes.

3. A. Will Henry return soon?

B. Yes, _he will_. _he'll_

return in a week.

4. A. Will we be ready soon?

B. Yes, _we will_. _will_

be ready in a little while.

5. A. Will Grandma and Grandpa arrive soon?

B. Yes, _they will_. _they'll_

_____ in 15 or 20 minutes.

6. A. Will the storm end soon?

B. Yes, _____. _it'll_

end in a few hours.

7. A. Will Kate be here soon?

B. Yes, _she will_. _she'll_

be here in a few minutes.

8. A. Will you get out soon?

B. Yes, _I will_. _I'll_

get out in a month.

30 **Activity Workbook**

WE'LL JUST HAVE TO WAIT AND SEE

1. Do you think Barbara ___will___ move to a new apartment soon?

   I don't know. Maybe ___she___ ___will___, and maybe ___she___ ___won't___.

2. Do you think Robert ___he___ like his new job?

   I don't know. Maybe ___he___ ___will___, and maybe ___he___ ___won't___.

3. Do you think ___you will___ drive to the beach this weekend?

   I don't know. Maybe I ___will___, and maybe _____.

4. Do you think ___you will___ be a famous scientist some day?

   I don't know. Maybe you ___will___, and maybe ___you___ ___won't___.

5. Do you think ___we will___ snow a lot this winter?

   I don't know. Maybe ___we will___, and maybe ___we___ ___won't___.

6. Do you think ___it___ ___will___ be a lot of traffic today?

   I don't know. Maybe ___it___ ___will___, and maybe _____.

7. Do you think you and Roger ___will___ get married soon?

   I don't know. Maybe ___we___ ___will___, and maybe ___we___ ___won't___.

8. Do you think the guests ___will___ like the fruitcake?

   I don't know. Maybe ___they___ ___will___, and maybe ___they___ ___won't___.

C WHAT DO YOU THINK?

Yes!   **No!**

1. What will Charlie bake for the party?

   Maybe _____ he'll _____ bake _____ cookies.

   I'm sure _____ he _____ won't bake _____ a cake.

2. What will Mom order at the restaurant?

   Maybe _she'll_ _order_ a sandwich.

   I'm sure _she_ _won't order_ a pizza.

3. Where will your parents go this evening?

   Maybe _they'll_ _go_ to a movie.

   I'm sure _they_ _won't go_ to a party.

4. What will you get for your birthday?

   Maybe _I'll_ _get_ a sweater.

   I'm sure _I won't_ _get_ a cell phone.

5. When will the train arrive?

   Maybe _it'll_ _arrive_ in an hour.

   I'm sure _it won't_ _arrive_ on time.

6. When will we finish our English book?

   Maybe _we'll_ _finish_ it in a few months.

   I'm sure _it won't_ _finish_ it next week.

D LISTENING

Listen and circle the words you hear.

1. won't / (want to)
2. (won't) / want to
3. (won't) / want to
4. (won't) / want to
5. (won't) / want to
6. (won't) / (want to)
7. (won't) / want to
8. won't / (want to)

E DIFFERENT OPINIONS

1. I think the weather will be nice tomorrow. Everybody else thinks _it'll be_ bad.

2. My wife thinks the guests will arrive on time. I think _they'll arrive_ late.

3. I think our daughter will be a lawyer. My husband thinks _she'll be_ an architect.

4. My parents think my brother Bob will buy a bicycle. I think _he'll buy_ a motorcycle.

5. I think we'll have a good time at the party. My husband thinks _it'll be_ a terrible time.

Listen. Then clap and practice.

A. I'll remember.

B. Are you sure?

A. Don't worry. I'll remember. You'll see.

A. He'll do it.

B. Are you sure?

A. Don't worry. He'll do it. You'll see.

A. She'll call you.

B. Are you sure?

A. Don't worry. She'll call you. You'll see.

A. It'll be ready.

B. Are you sure?

A. Don't worry. It'll be ready. You'll see.

A. We'll be there.

B. Are you sure?

A. Don't worry. We'll be there. You'll see.

A. They'll get there.

B. Are you sure?

A. Don't worry. They'll get there. You'll see.

1. A. What's Bruno going to make for breakfast this morning?

   B. _____He might make eggs_____, or

   _____he might make pancakes_____.

2. A. What time is Sally going to get up tomorrow morning on her day off?

   B. _She might get up at 10:00_, or

   or She might get up at noon.

3. A. When are your children going to clean their bedroom?

   B. _They might clean it today_, or

   they might clean it tomorrow.

4. A. What are you going to give your parents for their anniversary?

   B. _I might give a plant_, or

   I might give a painting for

   them.

5. A. What are you and your friends going to watch on TV tonight?

   B. _We might Watch game shows_, or

   We might Watch cartoon on

   TV tonight.

6. A. Where are Mr. and Mrs. Martinez going to go for their vacation?

   B. _They might fly to Manila_, or

   They might fly to Bankok,

   for their vacation.

7. A. Tell me, what are you going to do this weekend?

   B. _I might go to the beach_, or

   I might go to a museum

   for this weekend.

8. A. What's Arthur going to name his new cat?

   B. _He might name chester_, or

   He might name fluffy.

   for his new cat.

H BE CAREFUL!

1. Don't stand there!
   - (a.) You might get hit.
   - b. You might watch.

2. Put on your safety glasses!
   - (a.) You might hurt your ears.
   - b. You might hurt your eyes.

3. Don't touch those wires!
   - (a.) You might get a shock.
   - b. You might get cold.

4. Don't touch that machine!
   - (a.) You might get hurt.
   - b. You might get a helmet.

5. Watch your step!
   - a. You might finish.
   - (b.) You might fall.

6. Put on your helmet!
   - a. You might hurt your back.
   - (b.) You might hurt your head.

I LOUD AND CLEAR   W!

| winter   Wendy   walk   weather   work |

| wet   walk   waiter   won't   waitress |

1. _____Wendy_____ doesn't like to _____walk_____ to ___work___ in the _____winter_____ when the _____weather_____ is bad.

2. The ___waiter___ and the ___waitress___ ___won't___ ___be___ there. The floor is ___wet___!

| wife   wash   Walter   windows   want   weekend |

| wasn't   we   water   wanted   warm |

3. ___Walter___ and his ___wife___ ___want___ to ___wash___ their ___windows___ this ___weekend___.

4. ___we___ ___wanted___ to go swimming, but the ___water___ ___wasn't___ ___warm___.

break her leg	fall asleep	get fat	have a terrible time	rain
catch a cold	get a backache	get seasick	look terrible	step on her feet
drown	get a sunburn	get sick	miss our bus	

1. Jennifer won't go skating because

_____she's afraid she might_____

_____break her leg_____.

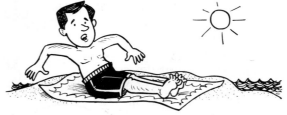

2. George won't go to the beach because

_____He's afraid He might_____

_____get a sunburn_____.

3. I won't go swimming because

_____I'm afraid, I might_____

_____drown_____.

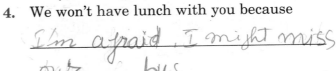

4. We won't have lunch with you because

_____I'm afraid, I might miss_____

_____our bus_____.

5. My mother and father won't go on the roller coaster because _____They're afraid_____

_____They might catch a cold_____.

6. Brian won't go dancing with Brenda

because _____he's afraid he might_____

_____step on her feet_____.

7. We won't go to a play because

_____We're afraid We might_____

_____fall asleep_____.

8. I won't go to Patty's party because

_____I'm afraid I might have a_____

_____terrible time_____.

9. Barry won't carry those boxes because

He's afraid he might get backache.

10. Sally won't go sailing because

She's afraid, she might get seasick

11. I won't eat dessert because

I'm afraid I might get fat

12. Helen won't take a walk in the park because

She's afraid she might get sick

13. We won't wash our clothes today because

We're afraid, it might rain

14. Fred won't get a short haircut because

He's afraid he might look terrible

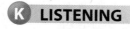

Track 20

K LISTENING 🔊

Listen and choose the correct answer.

1. **a.** He doesn't want to go on the roller coaster. *(circled)*
   b. He doesn't want to go to the doctor.

2. a. She doesn't want to go skiing.
   b. She doesn't want to go to the movies. *(circled)*

3. a. He doesn't want to go to a play.
   b. He doesn't want to go dancing. *(circled)*

4. **a.** She doesn't want to go skiing. *(circled)*
   b. She doesn't want to stay home.

5. a. He doesn't want to read a book.
   b. He doesn't want to take a walk in the park. *(circled)*

6. **a.** He doesn't want to go swimming. *(circled)*
   b. He doesn't want to go dancing.

7. a. She doesn't want to go skating.
   b. She doesn't want to go sailing. *(circled)*

8. a. He doesn't want to go to the library.
   b. He doesn't want to go to the beach. *(circled)*

9. **a.** She doesn't want to go to the party. *(circled)*
   b. She doesn't want to eat dinner.

10. **a.** He doesn't want to get a short haircut. *(circled)*
    b. He doesn't want to buy a small dog.

Listen. Then clap and practice.

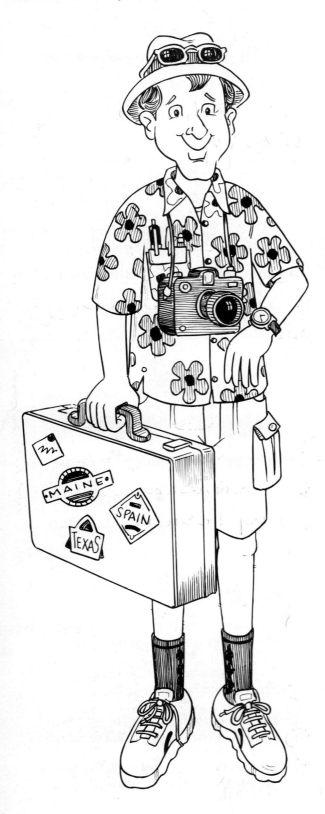

A. When is he going to   leave?

B. He might leave at   noon.

C. He might leave on   Monday.

D. He might leave in   June.

A. Where is he going to   go?

B. He might go to   Spain.

C. He might go to   Texas.

D. He might go to   Maine.

A. How is he going to   get there?

B. He might go by   train.

C. He might take the   bus.

D. He might take a   plane.

A. Who is he going to   go with?

B. He might go with   Ed.

C. He might go with   Peter.

D. He might go with   Fred.

A. What's he going to   do there?

B. He might see the   zoo.

C. He might take some   pictures.

D. He might write to   you.

Listen and fill in the words to the song. Then listen again and sing along.

cake	decide	go	her	make	Mexico	sweater	wide

I want to cook some dinner.

I don't know what to ___make___ 1.

I might make stew. I might make eggs.

I might just bake a ___cake___ 2.

I really don't know what to cook.

The choices are so ___wide___ 3.

I might cook this. I might cook that.

I really can't ___decide___ 4.

I'm planning my vacation.

I don't know where to ___go___ 5.

I might see France. I might see Spain.

I might see ___Mexico___ 6.

I really don't know where to go.

The choices are so ___wide___ 7.

I might go here. I might go there.

I really can't ___decide___ 8.

I'm buying Mom a present.

I don't know what to get ___her___ 9.

I might buy gloves. I might buy boots.

I might get her a ___sweater___ 10.

I really don't know what to get.

The choices are so ___wide___ 11.

I might get this. I might get that.

I really can't ___decide___ 12.

1. Henry's old sofa was soft. His new sofa is _____ softer _____.

2. Nancy's old briefcase was light. Her new briefcase is _____ lighter _____.

3. Bob's old living room was large. His new living room is _____ larger _____.

4. My old recipe for chili was hot. My new recipe is _____ hotter _____.

5. My old boss was friendly. My new boss is _____ friendlier _____.

6. Our old neighborhood was safe. Our new neighborhood is _____ safer _____.

7. Linda's old cell phone was small. Her new cell phone is _____ smaller _____.

8. Grandpa's old sports car was fancy. His new sports car is _____ fancier _____.

9. Cathy's old mittens were warm. Her new mittens are _____ warmer _____.

10. Billy's old school was big. His new school is _____ bigger _____.

11. My old job was easy. My new job is _____ easier _____.

12. Our old neighbors were nice. Our new neighbors are _____ nicer _____.

13. Richard's old watch was cheap. His new watch is _____ cheaper _____.

14. Dr. Green's old office was ugly. His new office is _____ uglier _____.

B WHAT'S THE WORD?

 Tima   Jim

1. A. Is Tim's hair short?

   B. Yes, but Jim's hair is _____ shorter _____.

2. A. Is Charlie's cat cute?

   B. Yes, but his dog is _____ cuter _____.

 Barbara    Betty

3. A. Is Debbie's dog fat?

   B. Yes, but her cat is _____ fatter _____.

4. A. Is Barbara busy?

   B. Yes, but Betty is _____ busier _____.

C THEY'RE DIFFERENT

1. Paul's parrot is talkative, but Paula's parrot is ___more talkative___.

2. Your roommate is interesting, but my roommate is ___more interesting___.

3. Sam's suit is attractive, but Stanley's suit is ___more attractive___.

4. Shirley's shoes are comfortable, but her sister's shoes are ___more comfortable___

5. George is intelligent, but his brother is ___is more intelligent___.

6. My daughter's hair is long, but my son's hair is ___more longer___.

7. Last winter was cold, but this winter is ___more colder___.

8. William is thin, but his father is ___more thinner___.

9. My children are healthy, but my doctor's children are ___more healthy___.

10. John's computer is powerful, but Jane's computer is ___more powerful___.

11. Barbara's boyfriend is handsome, but her father is ___more handsome___.

12. My teeth are white, but my dentist's teeth are ___whiter___.

13. Our neighbor's yard is beautiful, but our yard is ___more beautiful___.

D WHAT'S THE WORD?

1. A. This meatloaf is delicious.
   B. It's very good, but my mother's meatloaf
      is ___more delicious___.

2. A. Chicken is good for you.
   B. I know. But everybody says that fish
      is ___better___ for you.

3. A. This necklace is very expensive.
   B. You're right. But that necklace
      is ___more expensive___.

4. A. You're very energetic!
   B. Yes, I am. But my wife is ___more energetic___.

Activity Workbook 41

Across

4. My upstairs neighbor is friendly, but my downstairs neighbor is _friendlier_

7. Their baby is cute, but my baby is _cuter_.

8. Betty's blue dress is pretty, but her green dress is _prettier_

11. This bicycle is fast, but that bicycle is _____.

12. My old apartment was large, but my new apartment is _____.

13. Your dishwasher is quiet, but my dishwasher is _____.

Down

1. Our old rug was soft, but our new rug is _softer_

2. Yesterday it was warm, but today it's _warmer_

3. Their new house is small, but their old house was _smaller_

4. Tom's new tie is fancy, but his son's tie is _fancier_

5. My old tennis racket was light, but my new tennis racket is_____.

6. Bananas were cheap last week, but this week they're _cheaper_

9. The chili we ate last week was hot, but this chili is _hotter_

10. This picture is ugly, but that picture is _uglier_

F LISTENING track 23

Listen and choose the correct words to complete the sentences.

1. a. cooler
   b. cuter

2. a. smaller
   b. taller

3. a. more handsome
   b. more attractive

4. a. nicer
   b. lighter

5. a. fatter
   b. faster

6. a. friendlier
   b. fancier

7. a. more interesting
   b. more intelligent

8. a. bigger
   b. busier

cheap	delicious	fancy	small	talented	talkative

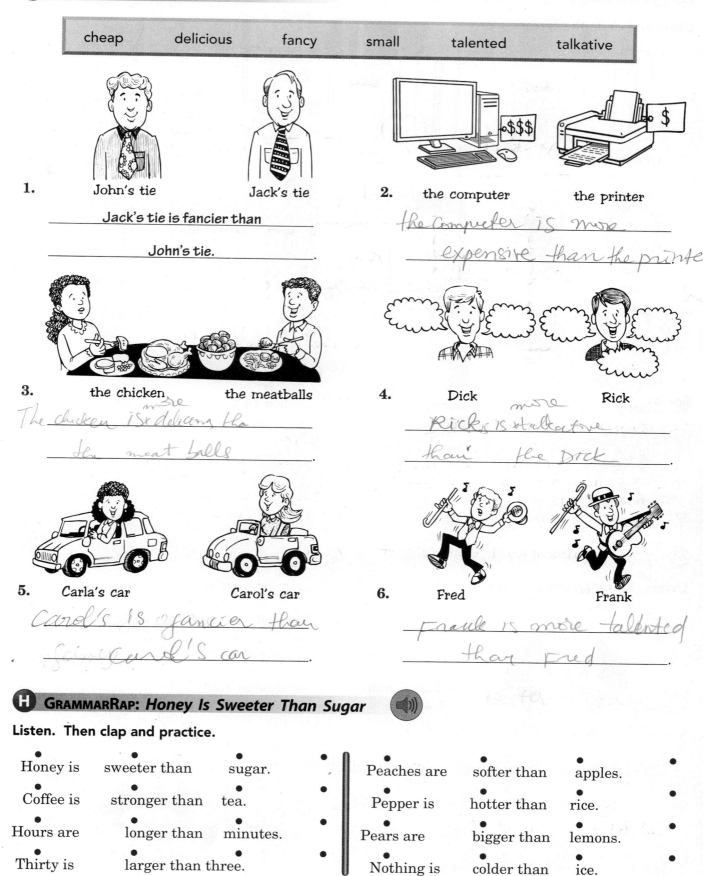

1. John's tie   Jack's tie

Jack's tie is fancier than

John's tie.

2. the computer   the printer

the computer is more

expensive than the printer

3. the chicken   the meatballs

The chicken is more delicious tha

the meat balls

4. Dick   Rick

Rick is more talkative

than the Drck

5. Carla's car   Carol's car

Carol's is fancier than

Carol's car

6. Fred   Frank

Frank is more talented

than Fred

H **GRAMMARRAP:** *Honey Is Sweeter Than Sugar*

Listen. Then clap and practice.

Honey is	sweeter than	sugar.
Coffee is	stronger than	tea.
Hours are	longer than	minutes.
Thirty is	larger than	three.

Peaches are	softer than	apples.
Pepper is	hotter than	rice.
Pears are	bigger than	lemons.
Nothing is	colder than	ice.

Listen and circle the correct answer.

1. yesterday   today

2.

3. Betty   Jane

4. Bob   Bill

5. Barry   Larry

6. science test   history test

7. Irene   Eileen

8. Ronald   Donald

capable

J **GRAMMARRAP:** *I Can't Decide* 🔊 Track 26

Listen. Then clap and practice.

I can't decide   who to go   out with.

Bob is more   interesting than   Bill.

Tom is more   handsome than   Tony.

And Frank's more   exciting than   Phil.

I can't decide   who to go   out with.

Alice is more   talented than   Anne.

Sue's more   attractive than   Sally.

And Jane's more   exciting than   Jan.

K WHAT SHOULD THEY DO?

call the dentist	fire him	rent a video
call the police	hire her	plant some flowers

shud

1. My garden looks terrible!

   You should plant some flowers.

2. Harvey has a very bad toothache!

   should call the dentist

3. My husband and I want to see a movie tonight.

   Should rent a video

4. A thief stole my daughter's new bicycle!

   should call the police

5. The people at the Ace company think that Jennifer is capable and talented.

   hire her
   thienust

6. Ms. Hunter is upset because her secretary falls asleep at work every day.

   should fire

L GRAMMARRAP: *Should They...?*   *track 27*

Listen. Then clap and practice.

A. Should he   call or should he   write?

B. He should   call   tomorrow   night.

A. Should I   keep it or give it   back?

B. You should wear it or give it to Jack.

A. Should I   stay or   should I   go?

B. Don't ask me.   I don't   know.

Activity Workbook 45

useful   exciting

1. Should I buy a van or a sports car?

I think _____ you should buy a van _____
because _____ vans are more useful than _____
_____ sports cars _____ .

(or)

I think _____ you should buy a sports car _____
because _____ sports cars are more _____
_____ exciting than vans _____ .

safe   fast

quiet   beautiful

2. Should she buy a bicycle or a motorcycle?

I think _____
because _____ safer than _____
_____ a motorcycle _____ .

3. Should we move to Weston or Easton?

I think _____
because _____ quitter _____
_____ .

is   warm a   fancy

ALAN LANE   talented   GEORGE GRAY   honest

4. Should he buy the fur hat or the leather hat?

I think _____
because _____
_____ .

5. Should I vote for Alan Lane or George Gray?

I think _____
because _____
_____ .

Mr. Hall   nice   Mr. Hill   capable

Patty   interesting   Pam   intelligent

6. Should we hire Mr. Hall or Mr. Hill?

I think _____
because _____
_____ .

7. Should he go out with Patty or Pam?

I think _____
because _____
_____ .

N WHAT'S THE WORD?

| mine | his | hers | ours | yours | theirs |

1. A. Is this Michael's cell phone?

   B. No. It isn't _____ his _____.

2. A. Are these your safety glasses?

   B. No. They aren't _____ ours _____.

3. A. Is this your sister's violin?

   B. No. It isn't _____ hers _____.

4. A. Is that Mr. and Mrs. Garcia's van?

   B. No. It isn't _____ theirs _____.

5. A. Is this my recipe for fruitcake?

   B. No. It isn't _____ yours _____.

6. A. Are these your son's sneakers?

   B. No. They aren't _____ his _____.

7.

   Is that your car?

   No. It isn't _____ mine _____.

O WHAT'S THE WORD?

1. You know, my parents aren't as sympathetic as your parents.

   Really? I think ((yours) your) are much more sympathetic than (my (mine)).

2. Robert's cookies aren't as delicious as his sister's cookies.

   Really? I think (him (his)) are much more delicious than (her (hers)).

3. Our computer isn't as fast as their computer.

   Really? I think ((ours) their) is much faster than ((theirs) them).

4. My pronunciation isn't as good as your pronunciation.

   Don't be ridiculous! (Your (Yours)) is much better than ((mine) my).

5. Jane's briefcase isn't as attractive as her husband's briefcase.

   Really? I think (her (hers)) is much more attractive than (him (his)).

Activity Workbook   47

DIFFERENT, BUT OKAY

1. My neighborhood (quiet) _____ isn't as quiet as _____ your neighborhood, but it's much (interesting) _____ more interesting _____.

2. Susan's sofa (fashionable) _____ isn't as fashionable as _____ her sister's sofa, but it's much (comfortable) _____ much more comfortable _____.

3. These apartments (modern) _____ aren't as modern as _____ our apartment, but they're much (large) _____ larger than _____.

4. George's car (powerful) _____ isn't as powerful as _____ Jack's car, but it's much (reliable) _____ more reliable _____.

5. The weather in our city (warm) _____ isn't as warm as _____ the weather in your city, but it's much (sunny) _____ sunnier _____.

6. My parents (talkative) _____ aren't as talkative as _____ my cousin's parents, but they're much (understanding) _____ more understanding _____.

7. The movie we rented last weekend wasn't (exciting) _____ as exciting as _____ this movie, but it was much (good) _____ better _____.

Q **YOU'RE RIGHT**

1. A. Ken's tie isn't as attractive as Len's tie.
   B. You're right. Len's tie is _____ more _____ attractive than Ken's tie _____.

2. A. Donald isn't as nice as Ronald.
   B. You're right. Ronald is _____ much nicer than Donald _____.

3. A. Larry isn't as lazy as his brother.
   B. You're right. Larry's brother is _____ much lazier than Larry _____.

4. A. English isn't as difficult as Russian.
   B. You're right. Russian is _____ much more difficult than English _____.

5. A. Julie's office isn't as big as Judy's office.
   B. You're right. Judy's office is _____ much bigger than hers _____.

6. A. My son isn't as talkative as your son.
   B. You're right. My son is _____ much more talkative than yours _____.

R GRAMMARRAP: *Ticket Mix-Up*

Listen. Then clap and practice.

Where's my   ticket?
Who has   mine?
I don't   want to
stand in   line.

Who has   hers?
Who has   his?
I wonder   where
my ticket   is!

He has   his.
I have   mine.
She has   hers.
Everything's   fine!

S GRAMMARRAP: *His Job Is Easy*

Listen. Then clap and practice.

His job is   easy.
Hers is,   too.
Mine's a more   difficult   job to   do.
His job's as   simple
As A B   C:
Mine   requires a   P H   D.

T WHO SHOULD WE HIRE?

A. Do you think we should hire Mr. Blake or Mr. Maxwell?

B. I'm not sure. Mr. Blake isn't as (lively) _____lively_____ [1]

as Mr. Maxwell, but he's much (smart) _____smarter_____ [2].

A. I agree. Mr. Blake is very smart, but in my opinion,

Mr. Maxwell is (talented) _much more talented_ [3] than
Mr. Blake.

B. Well, perhaps Mr. Blake isn't as (talented) _talented_ [4] as

Mr. Maxwell, but I think he's probably (honest) _more honest_ [5].

A. Do you really think so?

B. Yes. I think Mr. Blake is much (good) _____better_____ [6] for the job.
We should hire him.

A. Do you think we should hire Ms. Taylor or Ms. Tyler?

B. I'm not sure. Ms. Tyler isn't as (friendly) _friendly_ [7]

as Ms. Taylor, but I think she's much (intelligent) _more_

intelligent [8].

A. But Ms. Taylor is (talkative) _more talkative_ [9]

and (polite) _more politer_ [10] than Ms. Tyler.

B. That's true. But I think Ms. Tyler is (capable) _much_

more capable [11] than Ms. Taylor. I think we should hire her.

A. Do you think we should hire Mario or Victor?

B. I don't know. Mario's meatballs are (good) _____better_____ [12]

than Victor's, but his desserts aren't as (delicious)

delicious [13] as Victor's desserts.

A. That's true. But Mario's vegetable stew is (interesting)

more interesting [14] than Victor's. Also, Mario is

much (fast) _faster_ [15] than Victor. He's also

(nice) _nicer_ [16] than Victor.

B. You're right. I think we should hire Mario.

STUDENT BOOK
PAGES **49–58**

1. A. I think Alice is very bright.

   B. She certainly is. She's ___the___ ___brightest___ student in our class.

2. A. Your brother Tom is very neat.

   B. He certainly is. He's ___the___ ___neastest___ person I know.

3. A. Our upstairs neighbors are very nice.

   B. I agree. They're ___the nicest___ people in the building.

4. A. This dress is very fancy.

   B. I know. It's ___the fanciest___ dress in the store.

5. A. I think Nancy is very friendly.

   B. I agree. She's ___the friendliest___ person in our office.

6. A. Timothy is very quiet.

   B. I know. He's ___the quietest___ boy in the school.

7. A. Is their new baby cute?

   B. In my opinion, she's ___the cutest___ _____ baby girl in the hospital.

8. A. That dog is very big.

   B. It certainly is. It's ___the___ ___biggest___ dog in the neighborhood.

9. A. Your cousin Steven is very sloppy.

   B. He certainly is. He's ___the___ ___sloppiest___ person I know.

10. A. Morton Miller is very mean.

    B. I agree. He's ___the___ ___meanest___ man in town.

boring	generous	interesting	patient	smart	talented
energetic	honest ✓	noisy	polite	stubborn	

1. Jessica sings, dances, and plays the guitar. She's very _____talented_____.

   In fact, she's _____the most talented_____ person I know.

2. Mr. Bates gives very expensive gifts to his friends. He's very _the most generous_.

   In fact, he's _the most_ _____ person I know.

3. My Aunt Louise jogs every day before work. She's very _____energetic_____.

   In fact, she's ___the energetic_____ person I know.

4. Marvin always says "Thank you" and "You're welcome." He's very __polite__.

   In fact, he's __the most polite__ person I know.

5. Samantha always knows the answers to all the questions. She's very __smart__.

   In fact, she's __the smartest_____ person I know.

6. Edward isn't reading a very exciting novel. It's very _____.

   In fact, it's _____ book in his house.

7. Dr. Chen never gets angry. She's very _____.

   In fact, she's _____ person I know.

8. Mayor Jones always says what he thinks. He's very _____.

   In fact, he's __the most honest_____ person I know.

9. My next-door neighbor plays loud music after midnight. He's very __noisy__.

   In fact, he's __the_____ person I know.

10. I'm never bored in my English class. My English teacher is very __interesting__.

    In fact, she's _____ person I know.

11. My brother-in-law is always sure he's right. He's very __stubborn__.

    In fact, he's _____ person I know.

C WORLDBUY.COM

WorldBuy.com is a very popular website on the Internet. People like to shop there because they can find wonderful products from around the world at very low prices.

homework

1. (*attractive!*) Julie is buying a briefcase from Italy because she thinks that Italian briefcases are _____ the most attractive _____ briefcases in the world.

2. (*soft!*) David is buying leather boots from Spain because he thinks that Spanish boots are _____ the softest _____ boots in the world.

3. (*elegant!*) Francine is buying an evening gown from Paris because she thinks that French evening gowns are _____ the most elegant _____ gowns in the world.

4. (*modern!*) Mr. and Mrs. Chang are buying a sofa from Sweden because they think that Swedish furniture is _____ the most modern _____ furniture in the world.

5. (*warm!*) Victor is buying a fur hat from Russia because he thinks that Russian hats are _____ the warmest _____ hats in the world.

6. (*good!*) Brenda is buying a sweater from England because she thinks that English sweaters are _____ the best _____ sweaters in the world.

7. (*reliable!*) Michael is buying a watch from Switzerland because he thinks that Swiss watches are _____ the most reliable _____ watches in the world.

8. (*beautiful!*) Mr. and Mrs. Rivera are buying a rug from China because they think that Chinese rugs are _____ the most beautiful _____ rugs in the world.

9. (*delicious!*) Nancy is buying coffee from Brazil because she thinks that Brazilian coffee is _____ delicious _____ in the world.

10. (_____!) I'm buying _____ a phu oui dog _____ from _____ V.N _____ because I think that _____ dogs _____ s is/are _____ the smartest _____ in the world.

track 30   honework

Listen. Then clap and practice.

A.   What do you   think about   Kirk?

B.   He's the friendliest   person at   work!

A.   What do you   think about   Flo?

B.   She's the most patient   person I   know!

A.   What do you   think about   Pete?

B.   He's the nicest   boy on the   street!

A.   What do you   think about   Kate?

B.   She's the most talented   teacher in the   state!

A.   What do you   think about   Bob?

B.   He's the laziest   guy on the   job!

A.   What do you   think about   Frank?

B.   He's the most polite   (teller) at the   bank!

A.   What do you   think about   Nellie?

B.   She's the fastest   waitress at the   deli!

A.   What do you   think about this   kitty?

B.   It's the ugliest   (cat) in the   city!

homework

1. A. How do you like your new BMB van, Mr. Lopez?

   B. It's very powerful. It's much ___more___

   ___powerful___ than my old van.

   A. That's because the BMB van is _____

   ___the most powerful___ van in the world!

2. A. How do you like your Suny video camera, Mrs. Park?

   B. It's very lightweight. It's much _more_

   lightweight than my old video camera.

   A. That's because the Suny video camera is _____

   the most lightweight video camera in the world!

3. A. How do you like your new Inkflo printer, Ted?

   B. It's very efficient. It's much _more_

   efficient than my old printer.

   A. That's because the Inkflo printer is _____

   the most efficient printer in the world!

4. A. How do you like your Panorama fax machine, Jane?

   B. It's very dependable. It's much _more_

   dependable than my old fax machine.

   A. That's because the Panorama fax machine is _the_

   most dependable fax machine in the world!

5. A. How do you like your new Ever-Lite Flashlight, Henry?

   B. It's very bright. It's much _brighter_ than the
   flashlight I usually use.

   A. That's because the Ever-Lite Flashlight is _the_

   most bright flashlight in the world!

LISTENING 🔊

Listen and circle the words you hear.

1. (more comfortable)   the most comfortable
2. the best   (the worst)
3. (more energetic)   the most energetic
4. cheap   (cheaper)
5. (the most important)   more important
6. sloppier   the sloppiest
7. the worst   (the best)
8. lazier   (lazy)
9. (meaner)   mean
10. more honest   the most honest

G **PUZZLE**

boring   comfortable   delicious   good   honest   polite   safe   sloppy   small   ugly

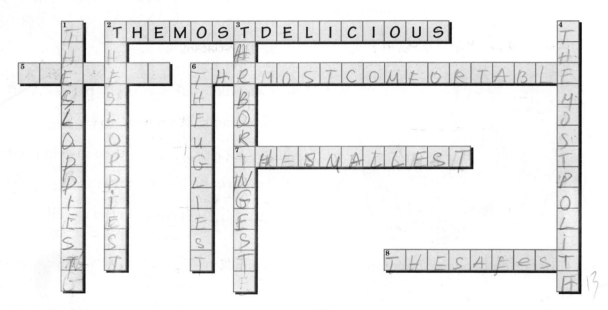

Across

2. Some people don't like this cereal. But I disagree. I think it's _the most_ cereal in the world. delicious

5. Even though Harry's Restaurant is the most popular restaurant in town, it isn't _good_.

6. This is my favorite chair. That's because it's _comfortable_ chair in the house.

7. My house isn't very big. In fact, it's _smallest_ house on the street.

8. Their old neighborhood was dangerous, but their new neighborhood is _the safest_ neighborhood in the city.

Down

1. Even though the salespeople at Ace Used Cars are the most helpful in town, they aren't _boring_

2. My son isn't very neat. In my opinion, he's _sloppiest_ person in our family.

3. I think golf is very interesting. But my wife disagrees. She thinks it's _the most_ game in the world. boring

4. Charles is never rude. In fact, he's _the polite_ boy in the school.

6. Emily's cat isn't very pretty. In my opinion, it's _the_ cat in town! ugliest

Fill in the words. Then read the sentences aloud.

worst	program	Andrew
terrible		actor

1. _____Andrew_____ is the _____worst_____
    _____actor_____ on this _____terrible_____
    TV _____program_____!

recipe	Carla's	fruitcake
recommend		better

2. I _recommend_ _Carla's_
    recipe for _fruitcake_.
    It's _better_ than yours.

energetic	friendlier	Robert
more		brother

3. _Robert_ is _energetic_
    and _more_ _friendlier_
    than his _brother_ Richard.

newspaper	writes	reads
Rita		morning

4. _Rita_ _reads_ the _newspaper_
    every _morning_, and she
    writes letters every afternoon.

perfume	birthday	sister
Ronald		thirtieth

5. _Ronald_ gave his _sister_
    flowers and _perfume_ for her
    thirtieth _birthday_.

powerful	bigger	more
neighbor's		car

6. My _car_ is _powerful_ and
    more _bigger_ than my
    neighbor's car.

Activity Workbook   57

again

A. Complete the sentences.

Ex. Will you be ready soon?

Yes, __I will__ . __I'll__
be ready in a few minutes.

Ex. Will your brother get home soon?

No, __he won't__ . He's at a baseball
game tonight.

1. Will the storm end soon?

Yes, __it will__ . __I'll__
end in a few hours.

2. Will Carol and Dave be in the office today?

No, __they won't__ . They're on vacation.

3. Will you return soon?

Yes, __I will__ . __I'll__
return in a little while.

4. Will Jane be in school tomorrow?

No, __she won't__ . She has a bad
cold.

5. Will you and Ray get out of work soon?

Yes, __I will__ . __I'll__
get out in half an hour.

B. Circle the correct answers.

1. I'm not going to fix that wire. I'm

afrid I (might) / should get a shock.

2. What do you think?

Might / (Should) I order the chicken or the fish?

3. When I grow up I (might) / should be a

dentist, or I (might) / should be a doctor.

4. It's going to rain. You might / (should) take

your umbrella.

C. Complete the conversations.

Ex. A. Are these Maria's gloves?

   B. No. They aren't __hers__ .

1. A. Is that your video camera?

   B. No. It isn't __mine__ .

2. A. Is that your son's computer?

   B. No. It isn't __his__ .

3. A. Is that Mr. and Mrs. Baker's house?

   B. No. It isn't __theirs__ .

4. A. Is this my recipe for meatballs?

   B. No. It isn't __yours__ .

D. Fill in the blanks.

Ex. Donald is __neater than__ Sam.
                  neat

1. Jane is __taller than__ Sarah.
              tall

2. Carl is __honester than__ Jack.
              honest

3. Centerville is __prettier than__ Lakeville.
                     pretty

4. The pie is __better__ the cake.
                good

5. Julie is __more dependable than__ John.
              dependable

E. Complete the sentences.

Ex. William (rich) __isn't as__ __rich as__ Walter, but he's much (happy) __happier__.

1. Ann's printer (fast) __isn't as fast as__ Betty's printer, but it's much (reliable) __reliable__.

2. Danny's dog (friendly) __isn't as friendly as__ Dorothy's dog, but it's much (cute) __cute__.

3. Howard (intelligent) __isn't as intelligent as__ Mike, but he's much (interesting) __interesting__.

4. My apartment (fashionable) __isn't as fashionable__ your apartment, but it's much (big) __bigger__.

5. Tom's furniture (expensive) __isn't as expensive as__ John's furniture, but it's much (attractive) __attractive__.

F. Fill in the blanks.

Ex. Brian is __the smartest__ person I know.
    smart

1. Marvin is __the quietest__ person I know.
    quiet

2. Uncle Bert is __the most hospitable__
     hospitable
person in our family.

again

3. We have __the largest__ apartment in the building.
    large

4. Mr. Peterson is __the most patient__ teacher in our school.
    patient

5. Mel is __the laziest__ person I know.
    lazy

G. Listen and circle the correct answer.

Ex.

Ronald

(Yes) / No

Fred

1.

Bob

Yes / No

Bill

2.

$6/lb.

Yes / (No)

$4/lb.

3. Moscow

32°

Yes / No

90°
Miami

4. Herbert

(Yes) / No

Steven

5. Pam

(Yes) / No

Patty

swedish citizen

A DID YOU KNOW?

Read the article on student book page 59 and answer the questions.

SIDE by SIDE Gazette
STUDENT BOOK
PAGES **59–60**

1. The ___d___ is in New York City.
   a. biggest igloo in the world
   b. longest car in the world
   c. biggest costume party in the world
   d. biggest subway station in the world

2. *Igloos* are _____.
   a. hotels that stay open in winter
   b. buildings made of hard snow
   c. hotels with many rooms
   d. Swedish hotels

3. More than 500,000 people _____.
   a. walk through Grand Central Terminal every day
   b. walk through the streets of Brazil in costume every day during Carnival
   c. stay at the Ice Hotel every year
   d. ride in the world's longest car every day

4. In Brazil people wear _____ to celebrate Carnival.
   a. costume parties
   b. bathing suits
   c. costumes
   d. evening gowns

5. The longest car in the world _____.
   a. has a waterbed to swim in
   b. is twenty-six feet long
   c. is a hundred meters long
   d. has 13 wheels on each side

6. According to this article, the Ice Hotel _____.
   a. has a swimming pool
   b. starts to turn to water when it's warm
   c. always has 150 guests
   d. is popular in the spring

B DO YOU KNOW? Your Country

Answer these questions about your country.

1. What's the largest city? _____ Montgomery ES largest city _____

2. What's the longest highway or road? _____

3. What's the most popular vacation place? _____

4. What's the most popular tourist sight? _____ Italy _____

5. What's the most popular food? _____

C DO YOU KNOW? The Longest and Shortest Words

Look in an English dictionary and in a dictionary in your language.

1. What's the longest word you can find in English? _____

2. What does it mean? _____

3. What's the longest word you can find in your language? _____

4. What does it mean? _____

D BUILD YOUR VOCABULARY! Prefixes

tiép dâu ngu

Complete the following words with the correct negative prefix.

1. _im_polite
2. _un_safe
3. _un_healthy
4. _in_expensive
5. _un_friendly
6. _dis_honest
7. _un_comfortable
8. _im_patient

E BUILD YOUR VOCABULARY! What's the Word?

Choose the correct word from the answers in Exercise D.

1. I really don't need another shirt, but I'll buy this one because it's _inexpensive_.
2. That car doesn't have any seat belts. Don't ride in it! It's _unsafe_!
3. Alex takes things in a store and doesn't pay for them. He's very _unhonest_.
4. There's too much sugar in those donuts. They're very _unhealthy_.
5. I don't sleep well at night because my bed is _uncomfortable_.
6. Luis wants to learn to speak English right away. He's _unpatient_.
7. Don't talk when you have food in your mouth! It's _unpolite_.
8. People think Gloria is _unfriendly_ because she's shy and likes to be alone.

F BUILD YOUR VOCABULARY! Prefix or No Prefix?

Choose the correct word from Exercise D—either with or without a negative prefix.

1. Butter and sugar aren't good for you, but vegetables are _healthy_.
2. Harvey always says thank you, but his brother Howard is very _unpolite_.
3. These shoes feel good on my feet, but those shoes are _uncomfortable_.
4. You can never believe anything Clara says, but her sister is very _honest_.
5. This dress doesn't cost a lot of money, but that dress is very _expensive_.
6. Daniel can wait for hours and never get upset, but his son Steven is very
   unpatient.
7. George never smiles or says hello, but his brother Robert is very _friendly_.
8. You won't have an accident in this car, but that car is _unsafe_.

BUILD YOUR VOCABULARY! What's the Prefix?

Can you guess the correct prefix? Write *un* or *in* before the adjective to
complete these conversations.

1. A. Is your landlord a kind person?

   B. No. My landlord is a very ____unkind____ person.

2. A. Do your parents wear fashionable clothing?

   B. No. They wear very ____unfashionable____ clothing.

3. A. Are the buses in your city reliable?

   B. No. They're always late. They're very ____unreliable____.

4. A. Is your apartment building in a convenient neighborhood?

   B. No. It isn't near any stores or bus stops. It's in a very ____unconvenient____ neighborhood.

5. A. Is that television program about the Pacific Ocean interesting?

   B. No. There isn't much information in the program. It's very ____uninteresting____

6. A. Are your neighbors hospitable?

   B. Not really. They never invite people to visit them. They're very ____unhospitable____.

H FACT FILE

Look at the Fact File on student book page 59 and answer the questions.

1. The Nile is a long _____.
   a. ocean
   b. desert
   c. mountain
   d. river

2. The largest ocean in the world is sixty-four million _____.
   a. miles long
   b. kilometers long
   c. square miles
   d. square kilometers

3. The Sahara is a large _____.
   a. ocean
   b. desert
   c. mountain
   d. river

4. The longest river in the world is 4,180 _____ long.
   a. feet
   b. miles
   c. meters
   d. kilometers

5. Mount Everest is _____ meters high.
   a. four thousand one hundred eighty
   b. twenty-nine thousand twenty-eight
   c. six thousand six hundred ninety
   d. eight thousand eight hundred forty-eight

6. There are 1000 meters in a kilometer.
   Mount Everest is almost _____ high.
   a. nine kilometers
   b. eighty-nine kilometers
   c. eight hundred ninety kilometers
   d. eighty-eight kilometers

7. The Nile is six thousand six hundred ninety
_____.
- a. miles long
- b. **kilometers long**
- c. miles high
- d. square kilometers

8. Sixty-four million square miles _____
165,760,000 square kilometers.
- a. is a little more than
- b. is much more than
- c. isn't as much as
- d. **is the same as**

9. The Sahara _____ nine million square
kilometers.
- a. is
- b. is less than
- c. **is more than**
- d. is much less than

10. The Pacific Ocean _____.
- a. is 165,760,000 kilometers long
- b. **is larger than the Atlantic Ocean**
- c. isn't as large as the Sahara desert
- d. isn't as large as the Atlantic Ocean

J "CAN-DO" REVIEW

Match the "can do" statement and the correct sentence.

C	1.	I can make an invitation.	a.	I'm positive!
i	2.	I can ask about future plans.	b.	Careful! Watch your step!
a	3.	I can express certainty.	c.	Would you like to go to the movies with me?
f	4.	I can express uncertainty.	d.	I think so, too.
b	5.	I can warn someone.	e.	Sorry we can't help you.
d	6.	I can agree with someone.	f.	I really can't decide.
h	7.	I can disagree with someone.	g.	May I help you?
j	8.	I can make comparisons.	h.	I disagree with you.
g	9.	I can offer to help a customer.	i.	What are you going to do this evening?
e	10.	I can apologize to a customer.	j.	The streets in your town are cleaner than the streets in our town.

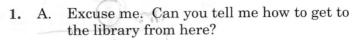

across from   on the right   walk up
between   on the left   walk down
next to

STUDENT BOOK
PAGES 61–70

SOUTH ST.

barber shop	library
clinic	toy store
shoe store	post office
bakery	book store
bank	drug store
high school	police station

1. A. Excuse me. Can you tell me how to get to the library from here?

    B. ___Walk up___ South Street and you'll see the library ___on the right___, ___across from___ the barber shop.

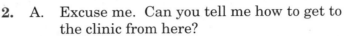

2. A. Excuse me. Can you tell me how to get to the clinic from here?

    B. _Walk up_ South Street and you'll see the clinic _on the left_, _next to_ the shoe store.

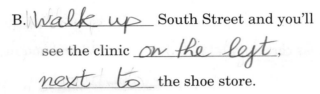

3. A. Excuse me. Can you tell me how to get to the toy store from here?

    B. _Walk up_ South Street and you'll see the toy store _on the right_ _across from_ the clinic.

4. A. Excuse me. Can you tell me how to get to the drug store from here?

    B. _Walk down_ South Street and you'll see the drug store _on the left_, _between_ the book store and the police station.

5. A. Excuse me. Can you tell me how to get to the high school from here?

    B. _Walk down_ South Street and you'll see the high school _on the right_, _next to_ the bank and _across from_ the police station.

across from
between
next to
on the left
on the right

walk along
walk down
walk up

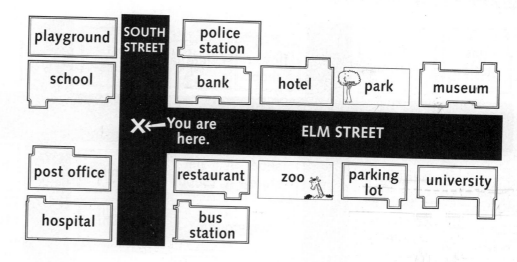

playground · SOUTH STREET · police station

school · bank · hotel · park · museum

X ←You are here. · ELM STREET

post office · restaurant · zoo · parking lot · university

hospital · bus station

1. A. Excuse me. Could you please tell me how to get to the university from here?

    B. _____Walk along_____ Elm Street and you'll see the university

    _____on the right_____ , _____across from_____ the museum.

2. A. Excuse me. Could you please tell me how to get to the park from here?

    B. _Walk along_ Elm Street and you'll see the park

    on the left , _next to_ the hotel.

3. A. Excuse me. Could you please tell me how to get to the police station from here?

    B. _Walk up_ South Street and you'll see the police station

    On the right , _across from_ the playground.

4. A. Excuse me. Could you please tell me how to get to the bus station from here?

    B. _Walk down_ South Street and you'll see the bus station

    on the left , _next to_ the restaurant.

5. A. Excuse me. Could you please tell me how to get to the zoo from here?

    B. _Walk along_ Elm Street and you'll see the zoo

    On the right , _between_ the restaurant and the parking lot.

C LET'S HELP MR. AND MRS. LEE!

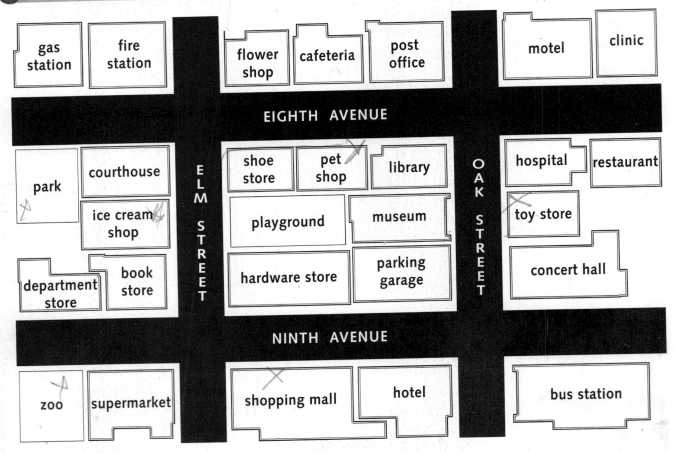

Mr. and Mrs. Lee are very busy today. They want to go several places with their children, but they don't know the city very well. They need your help.

1. They're at the shopping mall, and they want to take their children to the toy store to buy them a new toy. Tell them how to get there.

> _____Walk along_____ Ninth Avenue to Oak Street and _____turn left_____. _____Walk up_____ Oak Street and you'll see the toy store _____on the right_____, _____across from_____ the museum.

2. They're at the toy store, and now they want to take their children to the pet shop to buy them a dog.

> _____Walk up_____ Oak Street to Eighth Avenue and _____turn left_____. _____Walk along_____ Eighth Avenue and you'll see the pet shop _____on the left_____, _____between_____ the shoe store and the library.

3. They're at the pet shop, and they want to take their children to the ice cream shop for some ice cream.

_walk up_____ Eighth Avenue to Elm Street and _turn left_. _walk along_ Elm Street and you'll see the ice cream shop _next to_, _____ the courthouse.

4. They're at the ice cream shop, and they want to take their children to the zoo.

walk down Elm Street to Ninth Avenue and _turn right_. _walk along_ Ninth Avenue and you'll see the zoo _on the left_, _across from_ the department store.

5. They're at the zoo, and they're tired. They want to go to the park to rest.

Walk along Ninth Avenue to Elm street turn right, walk up Elm Street to Ninth Avenue turn left, you'll see the park on the left, next to the court house

6. They had a wonderful day, and now it's time to go home. Tell them how to get to the bus station.

Walk up Ninth Avenue, they'll see shopping Mall on the right, walk along Ninth Avenue the bus station on the right, across from concert hall

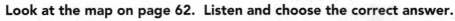

D LISTENING 🔊

Look at the map on page 62. Listen and choose the correct answer.

1. **a.** She was hungry.
   b. She wanted to buy a bird.

2. a. He wanted to look at paintings.
   b. He wanted to listen to music.

3. **a.** They wanted to read some books.
   b. They wanted to buy some flowers.

4. a. She wanted to buy some toys for her son.
   b. She wanted to visit her sick friend.

5. a. He wanted to buy some groceries.
   b. He wanted to look at the animals.

6. **a.** She was sick.
   b. She was hungry.

Listen. Then clap and practice.

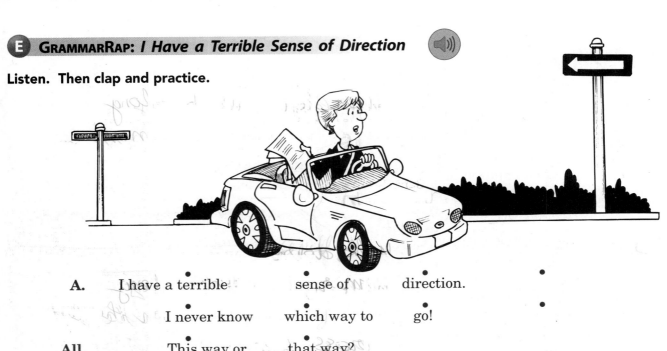

A.   I have a terrible · sense of · direction.
      I never know · which way to · go!

All.   This way or · that way?
      This way or · that way?

A.   I never know · which way to · go!
      I think that it's · that way, but · maybe I'm · wrong.
      I never know · which way to · go!

B.   I have a wonderful · sense of · direction.
      I always know · which way to · go!

All.   Turn · left!
      Turn · right!

B.   I always know · which way to · go!
      I know that it's · that way.
      I'm never · wrong!
      I always know · which way to · go!

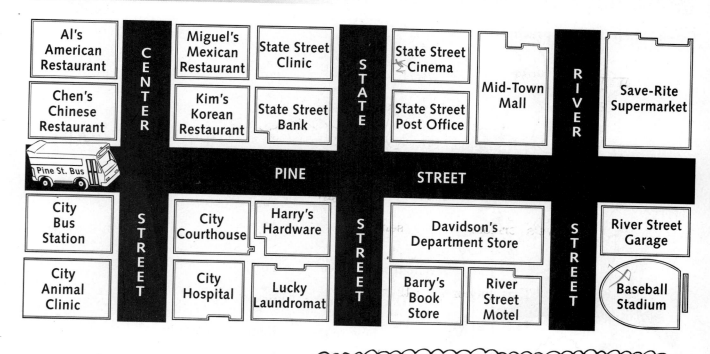

1. Jane is very hungry. She wants to have Mexican food for dinner. Tell her the best way to get to Miguel's Mexican Restaurant.

   __Take__ the Pine Street bus and __get off__ at __Center Street__. __Walk up__ __Center__ Street and you'll see Miguel's Mexican Restaurant __on the right__.

2. Ricky and his friends are late for the baseball game. Tell them the fastest way to get to the baseball stadium.

   Take the Pine Street bus and _get off_ at _River street_. _Walk down River_ Street and you'll see the baseball stadium _On the left_

3. Amanda and her mother are late for a movie. Tell them how to get to the State Street Cinema.

   Take the Pine Street bus and _get off_ at _STATE Street_. _Walk up STATE_ Street and you'll see the State Street Cinema _on the right_.

4. Tony's dog is sick. Tell him the shortest way to get to the City Animal Clinic.

   Take Pine St. Bus and get off at Center Street, walk down Center street you'll see City Animal clinic on the right, across from City Hospital

Listen. Then clap and practice.

Which way do we   go?

Does anybody   know?

Which way do we   go   from here?

Is it very   near?

Is it very   far?

I wish I   knew   where I left my   car!

Which way do we   go?

Does anybody   know

how to get   home   from here?

H GRAMMARRAP: *Turn Right!*

Listen. Then clap and practice.

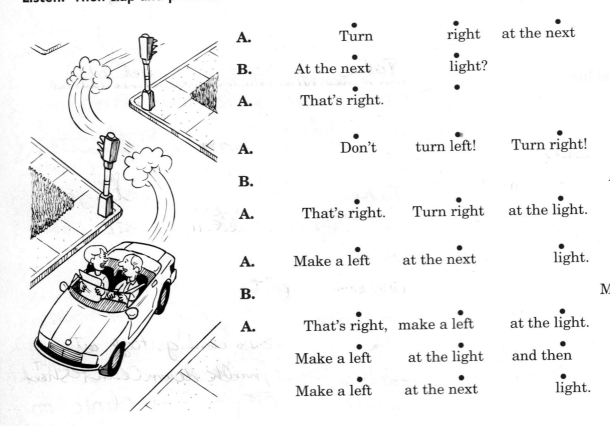

A.   Turn   right   at the next   light.

B. At the next   light?

A. That's right.

A.   Don't   turn left!   Turn right!

B.   At the light?

A. That's right.   Turn right   at the light.

A. Make a left   at the next   light.

B.   Make a left?

A. That's right,   make a left   at the light.

Make a left   at the light   and then   turn right.

Make a left   at the next   light.

I LISTENING: *Where Did They Go?*

DAY STREET

| shopping mall | | | | museum | | | | |
| bakery | bus station | hotel | | ice cream shop | motel | clinic | | scho... |

F I R S T   S T R E E T   S E C O N D   S T R E E T

BRIGHTON BOULEVARD

| barber shop | book store | drug store | | parking lot | toy store | gas station | | police station | bank |
| concert hall | zoo | | | flower shop | library | church | | shoe store | parking garage | statio... |

Day St. Bus   Bay Ave. Bus

BAY AVENUE

Listen and fill in the correct places.

1. He went to the _____bank_____.
2. She went to the _____library_____.
3. They went to the _____bakery_____.
4. She went to the _____museum_____.
5. They went to the _____zoo_____.
6. He went to the _____park_____.

J WHAT'S THE WORD?

| between | could | from | how | off | subway | turn | walk |
| certainly | excuse | get | left | please | take | up | |

A. _____Excuse_____ ¹ me. _____could_____ ² you _____please_____ ³
tell me _____how_____ ⁴ to _____get_____ ⁵ to the train
station _____from_____ ⁶ here?

B. _____Certainly_____ ⁷. _____take_____ ⁸ the
_____Subway_____ ⁹ and get _____off_____ ¹⁰ at Park Street.
Walk _____up_____ ¹¹ Park Street to Tenth Avenue
and _____turn_____ ¹² right. _____Walk_____ ¹³ along Tenth
Avenue and you'll see the train station on the
_____left_____ ¹⁴, _____between_____ ¹⁵ the post office
and the fire station.

Activity Workbook   **67**

ou think?

tely .

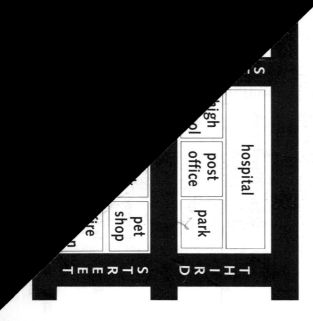

6. **A.** I think Fred is a dishonest card player.

B. I agree. He plays cards very _dishonestly_ .

7. **A.** I think Roger is a careless skier.

B. You're right. He skis very _carelessly_ .

8. **A.** Your sister Jill is a very slow eater.

B. I agree. She eats very _slowly_ .

9. **A.** Is Robert a _fast_ runner?

B. Yes. He runs very fast.

10. **A.** I think Ron is a _beautiful_ skater.

B. He certainly is. He skates very beautifully.

11. **A.** Is Margaret a _hard_ worker?

B. Yes, she is. She works very hard.

12. **A.** I think Frank is a _good_ baker.

B. I agree. He bakes very well.

B ANSWER

CAREFUL
(CAREFULLY) adv

1. Dr. Brown is a (careful / carefully) dentist. He cleans teeth very (careful / carefully).

2. We play golf (terrible / terribly), but we're (good / well) soccer players.

3. Mark dances (beautiful / beautifully). He's very (graceful adj / gracefully adv).

4. Richard isn't a very (good / well) driver. He drives very (fast / fastly).

5. I usually skate (safe / safely), but I was very (careless / carelessly) yesterday.

6. Anna bakes pies very (bad / badly), but her family eats her pies (polite / politely).

7. According to Sayako, you can't live (cheap / cheaply) in Tokyo. It's very (expensive / expensively).

8. Everybody in the office likes Rick. He's (reliable / reliably), and he works (energetic / energetically).

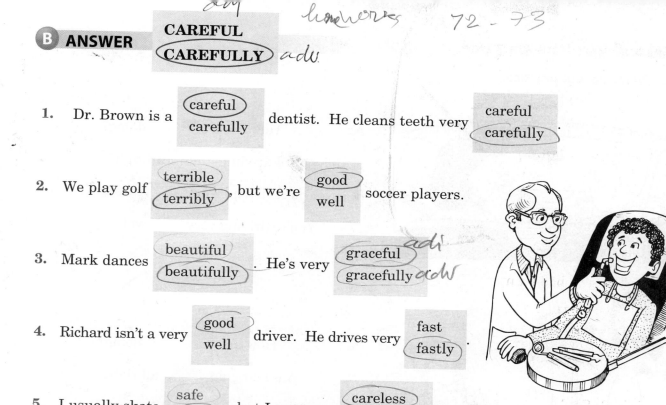

C LISTENING

Listen and circle the correct word to complete the sentence.

1. (slow)   slowly
2. beautiful   (beautifully)
3. dishonest   (dishonestly)
4. sloppy   (sloppily)

5. (accurate)   accurately
6. rude   (rudely)
7. safe   (safely)
8. reliable   (reliably)

9. soft   (softly)
10. cheap   cheaply
11. careful   carefully
12. patient   (patiently)

Listen. Then clap and practice.

A.   How am I   doing?

      Am I driving   all right?

B.   You're driving very   carefully.

      You're driving very   well.

A.   How am I   doing?

      Am I singing   all right? *adv*

B.   You're singing very   beautifully.

      You're singing very   well.

A.   How am I   doing?

      Am I dancing   all right? *adv*

B.   You're dancing very   gracefully.

      You're dancing very   well.

A.   How am I   doing?

      Am I working   all right?

B.   You're working very   hard.

      You're working very   well.

1. A. Am I jogging fast enough?
   B. You should try to jog

   _____ **faster** _____ .

2. A. Harold isn't speaking loudly enough.
   B. I agree. He should speak

   _____ *louder* _____ .

3. A. Am I typing carefully enough?
   B. Actually, you should type

   _____ *more carefully* _____ .

4. A. Is he translating accurately enough?
   B. No, he isn't. He should translate

   _____ *more accurately* _____ .

5. A. Rob, I don't think you're doing your
      work quickly enough.
   B. I'm sorry. I'll try to do my work

   _____ *more quickly* _____ .

6. A. I know I'm not dancing gracefully
      enough.
   B. You're right. You should dance

   _____ *more gracefully* _____ .

7. A. Am I cleaning the office well
      enough?
   B. Actually, you should clean it

   _____ *better* _____ .

8. A. Is the new mechanic working hard
      enough?
   B. I think he should work

   _____ *more hard* _____ .

9. A. Amanda, be careful! You aren't driving slowly enough!

   B. I'm sorry, Mr. Sanders. I'll try to drive _____ *more slowly* _____ .

RALPH SHOULD TRY HARDER!

Ralph has some problems. What should he do to make his life better?

1. Ralph always gets up very late.

   He should try to get up _____earlier_____.

2. He sometimes dresses very sloppily.

   He should try to dress _more neatly_.

3. He always eats breakfast very quickly.

   He should try to eat ____slower____.

4. He sometimes speaks rudely on the bus.

   He should try to speak _more polite_.

5. He usually works very slowly.

   He should try to work _more quickly_

6. He sometimes types carelessly.

   He should try to type _more accuratly_.

7. He plays his music very loudly every night.

   He should try to play it _more softly_.

G **WHAT SHOULD YOU TRY TO DO BETTER?**

I should try to _do more hard_ ....

I should try to _do a little harder_ ....

I should try to _do more carefully_ ....

I should try to _do more accurately_ ....

Listen and circle the words to the song. Then listen again and sing along.

Let's say you're a driver, a (careful) / carefully [1] driver who

drives very careful / (carefully) [2], as careful / carefully [3] drivers do.

Just try a little harder. You can find a way. Try to drive more careful / (carefully) [4] today.

Let's say you're a singer, a (beautiful) / beautifully [5] singer who

sings very beautiful / (beautifully) [6], as beautiful / beautifully [7] singers do.

Just try a little harder. You can find a way. Try to sing more beautiful / (beautifully) [8] today.

Let's say you're a dancer, a (graceful) / gracefully [9] dancer who

dances very graceful / gracefully [10], as (graceful) / gracefully [11] dancers do.

Try a little harder. You can find a way. Try to dance more graceful / (gracefully) [12] today.

Just try a little harder. That's what we always say. Sing a little strong / (stronger) [13]. Work a little

long / (longer) [14]. Do a little good / (better) [15] every day. Do a little good / better [16] every day.

I WHAT'S THE ANSWER?

1. If Helen _____ sick tomorrow, she'll go to work.
   - **(a.)** isn't
   - b. won't be

2. If the mechanic at Al's Garage fixes our car, _____ to the beach.
   - a. we drive
   - **(b.)** we'll drive

3. If _____ to your grandparents, they'll be very happy.
   - a. you write
   - **(b.)** you'll write

4. If Betty doesn't buy a VCR, _____ a CD player.
   - **(a.)** she buys
   - b. she'll buy

5. If you don't use enough butter, the cake _____ very good.
   - a. isn't
   - **(b.)** won't be

6. If _____ a course with Professor Boggs, I know it'll be boring.
   - a. I take
   - **(b.)** I'll take

7. If it _____ this Saturday, I think I'll go skiing.
   - **(a.)** snows
   - b. will snow

8. If you send me an e–mail, _____ right away.
   - a. I answer
   - **(b.)** I'll answer

9. If you _____ any more potatoes, I'll have rice with my chicken.
   - **(a.)** don't have
   - b. won't have

10. If the weather _____ good tomorrow, we'll play tennis.
    - a. is
    - **(b.)** will be

11. If I go on the roller coaster with you, I know _____ sick.
    - a. I get
    - **(b.)** I'll get

12. If you go there on your vacation, I'm sure _____ a good time.
    - **(a.)** you have
    - b. you won't have

J MATCHING

_d_	1.	If you stay on the beach all day,
_f_	2.	If you use fresh oranges,
_a_	3.	If you wear safety glasses,
_____	4.	If you follow my directions to the zoo,
_b_	5.	If you don't eat breakfast,
_____	6.	If you have a successful interview,

- **a.** you won't get hurt.
- **b.** you'll be hungry.
- **c.** you won't get lost. *Luiz*
- **d.** you'll get a sunburn.
- **e.** you'll get the job.
- **f.** the juice will be better.

1. If we _____ arrive _____ early, _____ we'll _____ visit your mother.

2. If _it rains_ this afternoon, I'll wear my new raincoat.

3. If the weather _will be_ good, my husband and I _____ go _____ sailing.

4. If David _____ plays _____ golf this weekend, _____ it'll be _____ a wonderful time.

5. If you _____ make _____ a lot of noise, your neighbors _will be_ upset.

6. If your son _____ takes _____ those wires, _he'll get_ a shock.

7. If _it'll be_ cold this Saturday, our family _____ go _____ skiing.

8. If Patty _____ eats _____ too much candy, _he get sick_ a stomachache.

9. If I _____ do _____ too many exercises, _I'll be_ tired tonight.

10. If we _'ll see_ a girl, _that's she_ her Patty.

11. If _there is_ a lot of traffic this morning, Nancy _____ will _____ probably be late for work.

12. If your parents _will go_ to Stanley's Restaurant on Monday, _it's_ _____ Italian food.

1. to suit. If he he'll party, goes new his the wear
_____ If he goes to the party _____ , _____ he'll wear his new suit _____ .

2. late she work. she'll be If bus, the misses for
if bus misses for she work , _she'll be late_ .

3. better. practice, I chess play I'll If
If I play chess , _____ , _I'll practice better._ .

4. buy go I I'll pie. an If bakery, the apple to
If I go to the bakery , _I'll buy an apple pie._

5. you sorry. If finish school, be you'll don't
If you don't finish school , _you'll be sorry_ .

6. Sam a works job. in good If he'll hard get school,
If Sam works hard in school , _he'll get a good job_ .

Complete the sentences any way you wish.

1. If the weather is bad this weekend, *I'll stay home*

2. If I go to bed very late tonight, *I'll be very tired*

3. If I don't eat dinner today, *I'll be hungry in the morning, tomorrow*

4. If my computer breaks, *I won't have the files*

5. If I make a terrible mistake at school or at work, *I'll fell down in my life*

6. If *they get holidays next week*, they'll go to a special restaurant tonight.

7. If *he graduate high school next year*, his mother will be very happy.

8. If *he doesn't visit them today*, his parents will be sad.

9. If *he files carelessly for his job*, his boss will fire him.

10. If *I speak impolitely to everyone*, my friends will be angry with me.

N **GRAMMARRAP:** *If You Leave at Six*

Listen. Then clap and practice.

If you leave at   six,
You'll be there at   eight.
If you don't leave   now,
You'll be very   late.

If you start work   now,
You'll be through at   seven.
If you wait 'till   noon,
You'll be busy 'till   eleven.

If you catch the   train,
You'll be home by   ten.
If you get there   late,
You'll miss dinner   again.

⊙ YOU DECIDE: *What Might Happen?*

1. You shouldn't worry so much.

   If you worry too much, you might *have headache*

2. Charlie shouldn't do his work so carelessly.

   If he does his work too carelessly, he might *lose his job*

3. Harriet shouldn't go to bed so late.

   If she goes to bed too late, she might *get up late in morning tomorrow*

4. Your friends shouldn't use the Internet so much.

   If they use the Internet too much, they might *get hurt their eyes*

5. You shouldn't talk so much.

   If *you talk too much*, you might hurt *your sorethroat*

6. Veronica shouldn't eat so much.

   If *she eats too much*, She might be *very fat*

7. Brian shouldn't buy so many expensive clothes.

   If *he buys too many expensive clothes*, He doesn't have *any money in his account*

8. Your friends shouldn't play their music so loud.

   If *they play their music too loud*, your neighbor next door *might call police*

9. Raymond shouldn't speak so impolitely to his boss.

   If *he speaks too impolitely to her*, She might *fire him right now* *boss*

10. You shouldn't speak so loudly.

    If *you speak so loudly*, you might *make noisy*

A. Please don't send me a lot of e-mail messages today!

B. Why not?

A. If you send me a lot of e-mail messages today, I'll
have to read them tonight.

If ___I have to read___ [1] them tonight, ____I'll____ [2] be tired
tomorrow morning.

And if ___I'll be___ [3] tired tomorrow morning, I'll fall asleep
at work.

If ___I'll fall sleep___ [4] at work, my boss ___will___ [5] be
understanding, and ___she'll___ [6] shout at me.

So please don't send me too many e-mail messages today!

A. Please don't play your music so loud!

B. Why not?

A. If you play your music too loud, the neighbors
will be upset.

If ___they___ [7] upset, they'll tell the landlord.

And if ___they tell___ [8] the landlord, ___he'll___ [9] get angry.

So please don't play your music so loud!

A. Please don't buy Jimmy a scary video!

B. Why not?

A. If you buy him a scary video, ___he'll___ [10] be afraid when he

goes to sleep. If ___he___ [11] afraid when he goes to sleep,

___he'll___ [12] have nightmares all night. If ___he have___ [13]

nightmares all night, he ___won't___ [14] get up on time. If

___he doesn't___ [15] get up on time, ___he'll be___ [16] late

for school. And if ___he is___ [17] late for school, ___he'll be___ [18]

miss a big test. So please don't buy Jimmy a scary video!

A.   Complete the sentences.

Ex. She's a beautiful singer. *adj*

  She sings very _____ **beautifully** _____. *adv*

1.   He's a terrible tennis player.

  He plays tennis _terribly_.

2.   She's a careful driver.

  She drives very _carefully_.

3.   They're bad cooks.

  They cook very _badly_.

4.   I'm a hard worker.

  I work very _hard_.

B.   Circle the correct answers.

1.   He isn't an ⟨honest⟩ / honestly player.

  He plays dishonest / ⟨dishonestly⟩.

2.   The bus is quick / ⟨quickly⟩, but it isn't

  quiet / ⟨quietly⟩.

3.   Mario is a ⟨good⟩ / well soccer player,

  but he doesn't run very good / ⟨well⟩.

4.   Alice usually drives safe / ⟨safely⟩, but

  last night she was ⟨careless⟩ / carelessly

C.   Complete the sentences.

Ex. Timothy talks too quickly.

  He should try to talk _{slower / ⟨more slowly⟩}_.

1.   Greta leaves work too early.

  She should try to leave work

  more lately

2.   Bobby speaks too impolitely at school.

  He should try to speak _more politely_

3.   Linda dances too awkwardly.

  She should try to dance _more_

  gracefully.

4.   Frank talks too softly.

  He should try to talk _more loudly_

D.   Complete the sentences.

Ex. If Jack _does_ his homework, his

  teacher _will be_ happy.

1.   If you _eat_ too many cookies,

  you will get a stomachache.

2.   If the music _is_ too loud,

  the neighbors _will be_ angry.

3.   If they _are_ a boy,

  I'll see him Steven.

4.   If _you're_ hungry tonight,
  I'll eat a small dinner.

E. Circle the correct answers.

1. If 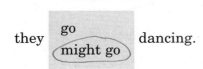 ~~we take~~ **(we'll take)** a vacation this

   year, we go **(we'll go)** to Hawaii.

2. If they **(feel)** ~~will feel~~ energetic tonight,

   they go **(might go)** dancing.

3. If you sing too loudly, you

   (get) ~~might get~~ a sore throat.

4. If it **(won't)** ~~doesn't~~ rain tomorrow,

   (I go) ~~I'll go~~ sailing.

F. Listen and fill in the correct places.

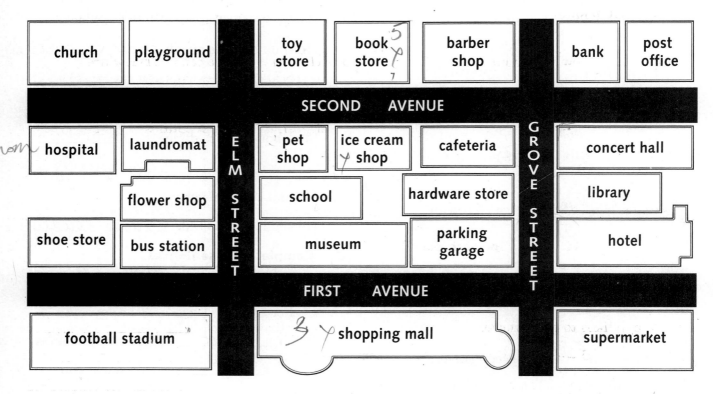

| church | playground | | toy store | book store | barber shop | | bank | post office |

SECOND   AVENUE

hospital	laundromat	E L M S T R E E T	pet shop	ice cream shop	cafeteria	G R O V E S T R E E T	concert hall
	flower shop		school		hardware store		library
shoe store	bus station		museum		parking garage		hotel

FIRST   AVENUE

| football stadium | shopping mall | | supermarket |

1. She went to the _ice cream shop_ .
2. He went to the _concert hall_ .
3. They went to the _shopping Mall_ .
4. He went to the _Hotel_ .
5. She went to the _book store_ .

80   Activity Workbook

A YOU'RE HIRED!

Read the article on student book page 81 and answer the questions.

1. The interview advice in this article is from
   _____.
   a. job applicants *(circled)*
   b. personnel officers
   c. supervisors
   d. presidents of companies

2. According to this article, you should talk
   about _____ at a job interview.
   a. the salary
   b. your family
   c. your skills *(circled)*
   d. the interviewer

3. According to this article, you should
   _____ when you're at a job interview.
   a. write a thank-you note
   b. shake your head firmly
   c. speak loudly
   d. smile *(circled)*

4. At an interview you shouldn't be _____.
   a. enthusiastic
   b. confident
   c. shy *(circled)*
   d. neat

5. *Make "eye contact"* means
   _____.
   a. look at the interviewer *(circled)*
   b. look at the floor
   c. take off your glasses
   d. look around the room

6. *Speak confidently* means talk _____.
   a. softly
   b. quickly
   c. honestly
   d. about how well you can do the job *(circled)*

7. If you don't have experience, tell the
   interviewer that _____.
   a. you have experience
   b. you can learn quickly *(circled)*
   c. you're sorry
   d. the job is easy and you don't need
      experience

8. The ten tips for a job interview are _____.
   a. the same everywhere in the world
   b. ten things applicants should never do *(circled)*
   c. ten things applicants should do
   d. ten things applicants always do

B BUILD YOUR VOCABULARY! What's the Job?

Choose the job that is right for each person.

designer	director	gardener	photographer	programmer	supervisor
6	5	1	3	2	4

1. Tanya likes to plant flowers.   *gardener*

2. Eric is good with computers. He studied computer science.   *programmer*

3. Suzanne loves to take pictures.   *photographer*

4. Sonya worked as an assembler. She wants a better factory job.   *supervisor*

5. Jean wants to make movies.   *director*

6. Richard loves to draw and paint.   *designer*

C BUILD YOUR VOCABULARY! Crossword

Across

1.

3.

4.

6.

7.

Down

2.

5.

4.

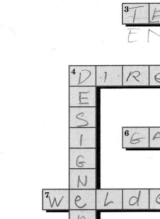

Crossword answers:
1 (Across) SUPERVISOR
2 (Down) INSPECTOR
3 (Across) TECHNICAL
(Down) EMP...
4 (Across) DIRECTOR
(Down) DESIGNER
5 (Down) WRITER
6 (Across) GARDENER
7 (Across) WELDER

D "CAN-DO" REVIEW

Match the "can do" statement and the correct sentence.

d	1.	I can get someone's attention.	a.	Can you recommend a good hotel?
f	2.	I can ask for directions to a place.	b.	I'll try to do better.
h	3.	I can ask for a recommendation.	c.	Thank you very much.
g	4.	I can give a recommendation.	d.	Am I speaking loud enough?
c	5.	I can express gratitude.	e.	You should type more carefully.
i	6.	I can ask for repetition.	f.	Excuse me.
e	7.	I can give feedback.	g.	If you go to bed late, you'll be tired tomorrow.
a	8.	I can ask for feedback.	h.	Can you tell me how to get to the library?
b	9.	I can promise to improve.	i.	Could you please repeat that?
j	10.	I can describe the consequences of actions.	j.	I think it's one of the best restaurants in town.

driving to the beach
fixing her fence
jogging
painting their house

playing basketball
riding his motorcycle
skateboarding
walking down Main Street

STUDENT BOOK
PAGES 83–92

1. What was Paul doing when it started to rain?

He was driving to the beach.

2. What was Diane doing when it started to rain?

walking down Main street

3. What were Mr. and Mrs. Adams doing?

jogging

4. What were you and your friends doing?

playing

5. What was Nick doing?

He was riding a motobike

6. What was Natalie doing?

She was fixing her fence

7. What were Tony and Mary doing?

They were painting

8. What were you and Mike doing?

They were skating
Skateboarding

9. What were YOU doing?

B WHAT WERE THEY DOING?

1. My children (bake) ____were baking____ a cake when I got home from work.

2. He (wear) _was wearing_ a helmet when he hit his head.

3. They (play) _were playing_ tennis when it started to rain.

4. She (ride) _was riding_ on a roller coaster when she got sick.

5. We (watch) _were watching_ a movie when we fell asleep.

6. He (sleep) _was sleeping_ at his desk when his boss fired him.

7. They (have) _were having_ an argument when the guests arrived.

8. I (chat) _was chatting_ online when the lights went out.

9. She (talk) _was talking_ to her friend when the teacher asked her a question.

C GRAMMARRAP: *Standing Around*

Listen. Then clap and practice.

We were singing and dancing and standing around,
Laughing and talking and standing around.

Susan was singing.
Danny was dancing.
Stella and Stanley were standing around.

Lucy was laughing.
Tommy was talking.
Stuart and Steven were standing around.

We were singing and dancing and standing around,
Laughing and talking and standing around.

D THE WRONG DAY!

Alan and his wife were very embarrassed when they arrived at the Franklins' house yesterday. They thought the Franklins' party was on Friday. But the Franklins' party wasn't on Friday. It was on Saturday!

bake	clean	make	sweep	vacuum	wash

1. What was Mr. Franklin doing when they arrived?

_____He was cleaning_____ the dining room.

2. What was Mrs. Franklin doing when they arrived?

She was vacuuming the living room rug.

3. What was Tommy Franklin doing?

He was sweeping the kitchen floor.

4. What was his sister Lucy doing?

She was washing the windows.

5. What were Mrs. Franklin's parents doing?

They were making spaghetti.

6. What were Mr. Franklin's parents doing?

They were baking cakes and cookies.

E LISTENING

Listen and choose the correct answer.

1. (a.) He was shaving.
    b. He was shopping.

2. a. She was skateboarding.
    (b.) She was skating.

3. a. They were sitting on the beach.
    (b.) They were swimming at the beach.

4. (a.) He was studying math.
    b. He was taking a bath.

5. a. We were reading.
    (b.) We were eating.

6. (a.) She was talking with her mother.
    b. She was walking with her brother.

7. (a.) He was taking a shower.
    b. He was planting flowers.

8. a. I was sleeping in the living room.
    (b.) I was sweeping the living room.

Activity Workbook **83**

fire extenguisha
bổ chữa lửa

F WHAT'S THE WORD?

1. When I saw her, she was getting
on
off
(into)

a taxi on Main Street.

2. Al was walking
(out of)
off
of

the park when

he fell.

3. I got
from
(off)
up

the bus and walked to

the bank.

4. We went
(into)
out of
at

a restaurant because

we were hungry.

5. Get
at
up
(on)

the subway at

Sixth Avenue.

6. Ann was skating
through
(along)
in

Center Street.

7. I'm getting
(out of)
off
up

the car

because I'm sick.

8. Susie got
(off)
to
at

the

merry-go-round.

G LISTENING

Listen and put the number under the correct picture.

5   2   6   3

8   4   1   7

GrammarRap: *I Called You All Day*

Listen. Then clap and practice.

A.   I called you   all day   today,

     But you never   answered your   phone.

B.   That's strange! I was   here from   morning 'till   night.

     I was home   all day   all alone.

A.   What were you   doing when I   called at   nine?

B.   I was probably   hanging my   clothes on the   line.

A.   What were you   doing when I   called at   one?

B.   I was probably   sitting   outside in the   sun.

A.   What were you   doing when I   called at   four?

B.   I was painting the   hallway and   fixing the   door.

A.   What were you   doing when I   called at   six?

B.   I was washing the   dog to get   rid of his   ticks.

A.   Well, I'm sorry I   missed you when I tried to   phone.

B.   It's too bad. I was   here. I was   home   all alone.

NOBODY WANTS TO

| myself | yourself | himself | herself | ourselves | yourselves | themselves |

1. Nobody wants to go fishing with me.

   I'll have to go fishing by _____myself_____.

2. Nobody wants to drive to the beach with her.

   She'll have to drive to the beach by ____herself____.

3. Nobody wants to go to the circus with us.

   We'll have to go to the circus by ____ourselves____.

4. Nobody wants to go to the playground with you.

   You'll have to go to the playground by ____yourself____.

5. Nobody wants to eat lunch with them.

   They'll have to eat lunch by ____themselves____.

6. Nobody wants to watch the video with him.

   He'll have to watch the video by ____himself____.

7. Nobody wants to play volleyball with you and your brother.

   You'll have to play volleyball by ____yourselves____.

WHAT'S THE WORD?

1. My husband and I like to have a picnic
   by _____.
   (a.) ourselves
   b. ourself

2. Bobby likes to drink his milk by _____.
   a. hisself
   (b.) himself

3. My mother and father drove to the
   mountains by _____.
   a. themself
   (b.) themselves

4. My grandmother likes to take a walk in
   the park by _____.
   (a.) herself
   b. herselves

5. I like to do my homework by _____.
   (a.) myself
   b. yourself

6. You and your brother like to fix the car by
   _____.
   a. yourself
   (b.) yourselves

K WHAT HAPPENED?

| bite | cook | drop | fall | | have | lose | ride | | shave | steal | walk |
| burn | cut | faint | get on | | hurt | paint | roller-blade | | ski | trip | watch |

1. Jane ___(tripped)___ while ___she___ ___was walking___ down the stairs.

2. A dog _bite_ Johnny while _he_ _was riding_ his bicycle.

3. Sam _watched TV_ while _he_ _was fainting_ a scary video.

4. Someone _steal_ our car while _we_ _were having_ dinner at a restaurant.

5. Diane _dropped_ her packages while _she was getting on_ the bus.

6. I _cut_ myself while _I was shaving_ .

7. Mr. and Mrs. Ling _burned_ themselves while _they were cooking_ on the barbecue.

8. Brian _lost_ his wallet while _he was using roller-blade_

9. We _skied_ ourselves while _we were hurting_ .

10. A can of paint _fell_ on them while _they were painting_ their house.

L WHAT'S THE WORD?

1. We were walking [through / into / (up)] the stairs.

2. They were driving [out of / (over) / down] a bridge.

3. A heavy book fell [(on) / out of / along] me.

4. They were walking [on / along / (out of)] the bank.

5. She was working [into / (at) / over] her office.

6. Let's go jogging [(through) / along / over] the park!

7. Don't walk [(under) / over / in] a ladder!

M LISTENING

Listen and choose the correct answer.

1. (a.) She lost her new boot.
   b. She lost her new suit.

2. a. He hurt himself while he was cooking.
   (b.) He burned himself while he was cooking.

3. a. While they were walking into the bank.
   (b.) While they were walking out of the park.

4. a. Someone stole our new fan.
   (b.) Someone stole our new van.

5. (a.) I dropped my new CD player.
   b. I dropped my new DVD player.

6. a. A dog bit him while he was working.
   (b.) A dog bit him while he was walking.

7. a. We were driving under a bridge.
   (b.) We were driving over a bridge.

8. (a.) She tripped and fell on the kitchen floor.
   b. She tripped and fell near the kitchen door.

9. a. While they were walking down the stairs.
   (b.) While they were walking up the stairs.

10. (a.) She was cooking on the barbecue.
    b. She was walking on Park Avenue.

11. (a.) I cut myself while I was chopping.
    b. I cut myself while I was shopping.

12. a. He waited at the bus stop.
    (b.) He fainted at the bus stop.

Listen. Then clap and practice.

A. Does she need a ladder? B. No, she doesn't.

She can reach the top shelf by herself.

All. She can reach the top shelf by herself. Look at that!

She can reach the top shelf by herself!

A. Does he need a cart? B. No, he doesn't.

He can carry all the luggage by himself.

All. He can carry all the luggage by himself. Look at that!

He can carry all the luggage by himself!

A. Do you need a calculator? B. No, I don't.

I can add all these numbers by myself.

All. You can add all those numbers by yourself. Look at that!

You can add all those numbers by yourself!

Fill in the words. Then read the sentences aloud.

e-mail   Greece   reading
niece   keypal

1. My ___niece___ Louise is ___reading___
    an ___e-mail___ from her ___keypal___
    in ___Greece___ .

himself   building   William   his
tripped   office

2. ___William___ ___tripped___ and hurt
    ___himself___ in front of ___his___
    ___office___ ___building___ .

cheese   asleep   fifteen   cookies
Steve   three

3. ___Steve___ fell ___asleep___ at ___three___
    ___fifteen___ . He ate too many ___cookies___
    and too much ___cheese___ .

busy   children   Hill   sick
clinic   city

4. Dr. ___Hill___ is very ___busy___ at his
    ___clinic___ . A lot of ___children___
    in the ___city___ are ___sick___ today.

beach   she's   Lee   Tahiti
CDs   sleeping

5. Mr. and Mrs. ___Lee___ are on the ___beach___
    in ___Tahiti___ . He's ___sleeping___ , and
    ___she's___ listening to ___CDs___ .

sandwich   isn't   milk   little
spilled   sister

6. My ___sister___ ___little___ Jill ___isn't___
    very happy. She dropped her ___sandwich___
    and ___spilled___ her ___milk___ .

A WHAT'S THE WORD?

could	can
couldn't	can't

1. Before I took lessons from Mrs. Rossini, I _____couldn't_____ play the violin very well.

   Now I _____can_____ play the violin beautifully.

2. I'm sorry you _____couldn't_____ go to the beach with us last weekend. Maybe you

   _____can_____ go with us next weekend.

3. When I first arrived in this country, I was frustrated because I _____couldn't_____ speak

   English. Now I'm happy because I _____can_____ speak English very well.

4. We _____couldn't_____ hear him because he spoke too softly.

5. We really want to fire Howard, but we _____couldn't_____. His father is president of the
   company.

6. My parents tell me that I was a very bright little girl. According to them, I _____couldn't_____

   read when I was two years old, and I _____could_____ write when I was three years old.

7. We _____couldn't_____ move the refrigerator by ourselves because it was too heavy.

8. I _____couldn't_____ go to work yesterday because I was sick. But today I'm feeling much

   better. I'm sure I _____can_____ go to work tomorrow.

9. Michael _____couldn't_____ go to lunch with his co-workers because he was too busy.

10. I _____couldn't_____ play basketball when I was in high school because I was too short. But

    I wasn't upset because I _____can_____ play on the baseball team.

11. I'm disappointed. We _____couldn't make_____ barbecue tonight. It's raining.

12. I _____couldn't_____ ask my boss for a raise. I was too nervous.

Listen. Then clap and practice.

A.   She tried on the skirt, but she   couldn't zip it   up.

B.   Was it too   small?

A.   Much too   small.

A.   She tried on the shoes, but she   couldn't keep them   on.

B. Were they too   big?

A.   Much too   big.

A.   He tried to   talk, but he   couldn't say a   word.

B.   Was he too   nervous?

A.   Much too   nervous.

A.   She sat at the   table, but she   couldn't eat a   thing.

B. Was she too   excited?

A.   Much too   excited.

A.   He went to the   lecture, but he   couldn't stay   awake.

B.   Was he too   tired?

A.   Much too   tired.

A.   She took the   course, but she   couldn't pass the   test.

B.   Was it too   hard?

A.   Much too   hard.

C YOU DECIDE: *Why Weren't They Able to?*

> | wasn't able to | weren't able to |

1. Daniel _____ **wasn't able to** _____ lift the package

   because _____ **it was too heavy** _____ (*or*)

   _____ **he was too tired** _____ (*or*)

   _____ **he was too weak.**

2. Barbara _wasn't able to_ go to work yesterday because _it was too windy or she was too tired_

3. My grandparents _weren't able to_ finish their dinner because _it was too spicy or they were too nervous_

4. Jim _wasn't able to_ buy the car he wanted because _it wass too expensive or he was too poor_

5. I _wasn't able to_ get on the bus this morning because _it was too crowed or I was too late_

6. The students in my class _weren't able to_ solve the puzzle because _it was too hard or they were too lazy_

7. Maria _wasn't able to_ fall asleep last night because _it was too late or she was too sad (tired)_

8. My brother _wasn't able to_ wear my tuxedo to his wedding because _it was too smell or he was too fat_

9. We _weren't able to_ go sailing last weekend because _it was too windy or we were too crowed_

10. Robert _was able to_ say "I love you" to his girlfriend because _it was too nervous or he was too shy_

D WHAT'S THE WORD?

| { could
was/were able to } | { couldn't
wasn't/weren't able to } | had to |

1. The bus was very crowded this morning. I _{couldn't / wasn't able to}_ sit. I ___had to___ stand.

2. Carlos was very disappointed. He ___couldn't___ take his daughter to the circus on Saturday because he ___had to___ work overtime.

3. When I was young, I was very energetic. I ___could___ run five miles every day.

4. When Judy was ten years old, her family moved to a different city. She was sad because she ___couldn't___ see her old friends very often.

5. When I was a little boy, I was upset because my older brothers ___were able to___ go to bed late, but I ___couldn't be late___, I ___had to___ go to bed at 7:30 every night.

6. We're sorry we ___couldn't___ go to the tennis match with you yesterday. We ___had to___ take our car to the mechanic.

7. When I was a teenager, I was very athletic. I ___could___ play baseball, and I ___could___ play football. But I was a terrible singer and dancer. I ___wasn't able to___ sing, and I ___wasn't able to___ dance.

8. My wife and I ___weren't able to___ go to our son's soccer game after school yesterday because we ___had to___ meet with our lawyer.

9. Brian was upset because he wanted to have long hair, but he ___wasn't able to___. He ___had to___ go to the barber every month because his parents liked very short hair.

YOU DECIDE: *Why Didn't They Enjoy Themselves?*

myself ourselves yourself yourselves himself themselves herself	couldn't wasn't able to weren't able to

1. I didn't enjoy _____myself_____ at the beach yesterday.

   It was very windy, and I ___couldn't go swimming___ *(or)*

   _____wasn't able to go sailing_____

2. Jim and his friends didn't enjoy _themselves_ at the movie yesterday. It was

   very scary, and they _couldn't understand it or wasn't able to get off_

3. Nancy didn't enjoy ____herself____ at the museum. It was very crowded, and she

   couldn't watch the pictures or wasn't able to take photos

4. Edward didn't enjoy ____himself____ at the restaurant last night. The food was

   very spicy, and he _couldn't eat his dinner or wasn't able to swallow_

5. I didn't enjoy ____myself____ at the circus last Friday. It was very noisy, and I

   couldn't run around or wasn't able to listen music

6. We didn't enjoy ____ourselves____ on our vacation last winter. We got sick, and we

   couldn't go outside or weren't able to visit

F **WHAT'S THE WORD?**

1. Walter was pleased. He didn't have to call
   the plumber. He ____ fix the sink himself.
   a. couldn't
   b.) was able to

2. I ____ get to work on time this morning
   because the bus was late.
   a. was able to
   b.) couldn't

3. I missed the company picnic yesterday
   because I ____ go to the eye doctor.
   a.) had to
   b. wasn't able to

4. We ____ finish our dinner because we were
   too full.
   a. could
   b.) weren't able to

5. I forgot my briefcase, and I ____ to go
   back home and get it.
   a. wasn't able to
   b.) had

6. We ____ fall asleep last night. Our
   neighbors played their music very loudly.
   a.) couldn't
   b. were able to

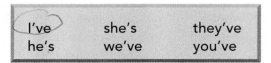

I've   she's   they've
he's   we've   you've

got to

Tomorrow afternoon David is moving to a new apartment next door. He asked a lot of people to help him, but unfortunately, everybody is busy tomorrow afternoon, and nobody will be able to help him. They all have things they've got to do.

1. His friend Bob won't be able to help him.

   _____**He's got to**_____ take his daughter to the doctor.

2. His friend Sandra won't be able to help him.

   (has)
   _____She's got to_____ drive her brother to the train station.

3. I'm sorry. I won't be able to help you.

   _____I've got to_____ take care of my neighbor's little boy.

4. Tom and I won't be able to help you, either.

   _____I've got to_____ stay home and wait for the plumber.

5. David's brother won't be able to help him.
   (has)
   _____He's got to_____ study for an important English test.

6. David's cousins won't be able to help him.

   _____ go to baseball practice.

7. We're really sorry, David.

   Unfortunately, _____ move to your new apartment by yourself.

H MY FRIEND LISA

will / won't be able to

My friend Lisa is an active, energetic person.

1. She goes jogging every morning.
2. She rides her bicycle to school every day.
3. She plays tennis on the school team.
4. She swims every afternoon.
5. She does exercises every evening.

She's also very talented and capable.

6. She plays the violin.
7. She bakes delicious cakes and cookies.
8. She makes her own clothes.
9. She fixes her computer when it's broken.

Last week on Friday the 13th Lisa went skating, and unfortunately, she broke her leg. The doctor says she'll have to rest her leg all month. Lisa is very upset.

1. _She won't be able to go jogging every morning._
2. _____
3. _____
4. _____
5. _____

Fortunately, there are many things that Lisa WILL be able to do.

6. _She'll be able to play the violin._
7. _____
8. _____
9. _____

I THEY'LL BE ABLE TO

couldn't   will be able to

1. My daughter ____couldn't____ go to her ballet lesson today, but I'm sure ___she'll be able to___ go next week.

2. We _____ assemble our new lamp yesterday. I hope _____ assemble it today.

3. Bill _____ go to football practice today. He thinks _____ go to football practice tomorrow.

4. I _____ fall asleep last night. I hope _____ fall asleep tonight.

J THEY WON'T BE ABLE TO

| won't be able to | have/has got to |

1. I'm sorry. I _____won't be able to_____ cook dinner tonight.
   _____I've got to_____ work overtime.

2. I'm terribly sorry. My daughter _____ baby-sit
   this afternoon. _____ practice the violin.

3. My children _____ eat ice cream at the party.
   Their doctor told them_____ eat fruit for dessert.

4. I'm really upset. My father _____ lend us money
   because _____ buy a new van.

5. Unfortunately, my husband and I _____ play golf
   with you today. _____ take our dog to the vet.

K LISTENING

Listen to each story, and then choose the correct answers to the questions you hear.

William's New Apartment

1. a. He was able to open his living room windows.
   b. He couldn't open his living room windows. *(circled)*

2. a. The lights in his apartment went out.
   b. His apartment is too bright.

3. a. He won't be able to cook dinner.
   b. He'll be able to watch his favorite programs on TV.

Mr. and Mrs. Clark's New Computer

4. a. They could assemble their computer easily.
   b. They weren't able to assemble their computer easily.

5. a. Their computer crashed.
   b. They used their new computer.

6. a. They'll be able to call their grandchildren.
   b. They won't be able to send any e-mail to their grandchildren.

GRAMMARRAP: *Were You Able to?*

Listen. Then clap and practice.

A. Were you able to   leave   early   last night?

B.   No. I had to   work until   seven.

A. Were you able to   get to the   office   on time?

B.   No.   I couldn't get there 'till   eleven.

A. Were you able to   take the   six o'clock   bus?

B.   No. I had to   wait until   eight.

A. Were you able to   get to the   meeting   on time?

B.   No.   I had to walk in   late.

M **GRAMMARRAP:** *They Won't Be Able to*

Listen. Then clap and practice.

A. Will you be able to   join us for   dinner?

B.   No, I won't. I've   got to work   late.

A. Will he be able to   meet us   tomorrow?

B.   No, he won't. He's   got to see   Kate.

A. Will she be able to   come to the   meeting?

B.   No, she won't. She's   got to call   Jack.

A. Will they be able to   go on the   sightseeing   trip?

B.   No, they won't. They've   got to   unpack.

Listen and fill in the words to the song. Then listen again and sing along.

day	do	go	no	play	to	today

My friend Jim called the other _____day_____ 1.

He said, "Would you like to see a play _____2?"

I didn't really want to _____3, so this is how I told him _____4.

I'm afraid I won't be able _____5. I have a lot of things to _____6.

I've got to wash my clothes and clean my house today.

But thank you for the invitation. I want to express my appreciation.

I'm sure that we'll be able to see a _____7 another _____8.

My friend Bob called the other _____9.

He said, "Would you like to roller-skate _____10?"

I didn't really want to _____11, so this is how I told him _____12.

I'm afraid I won't be able _____13. I have a lot of things to _____14.

I've got to paint my house and bathe my cat today.

But thank you for the invitation. I want to express my appreciation.

I'm sure that we'll be able to roller-skate another day.

I'm sure that we'll be able to.

I'm sure that we'll be able to.

✔ CHECK-UP TEST: Chapters 9–10

A. Complete the sentences.

Ex. She (wash) ___was washing___ her hair when the lights went out.

1. We (play) _____ basketball when it started to rain.

2. I (drive) _____ my car when I crashed into a tree.

3. They (jog) _____ in the park when the snow began.

4. Marvin cut himself while he (shave) _____ this morning.

5. A thief stole our car while we (read) _____ in the library.

6. She fell on the sidewalk while she (ride) _____ her bicycle.

7. I got paint all over myself while I (sit) _____ on a bench in the park.

B. Fill in the blanks.

Ex. I enjoyed ___myself___ at the museum.

1. We didn't enjoy _____ at the concert.

2. Richard burned _____ while he was cooking on the barbecue.

3. Did you and your husband enjoy _____ at the party?

4. Did you fix the VCR by _____, or did your wife help you?

5. Mr. and Mrs. Lopez cut _____ while they were fixing their fence.

6. Nobody went skating with Kate. She had to go skating by _____.

C. Circle the correct answers.

1. When I saw Jill, she was getting [off / of / in] a bus.

2. I usually get [at / up / on] the subway at First Street.

3. When the teacher walked [out of / off / of] the room, everybody started to talk.

4. We run [through / off / on] the park every day.

5. They were walking [from / into / at] the bank when I saw them.

6. The mail carrier [could / couldn't / can't] deliver our mail yesterday because our dog bit him.

7. I'm sorry you [couldn't / were able to / won't be able to] go to the baseball game with us tomorrow.

(continued)

8. When I was a teenager, I wanted to go out with my friends every night, but I

could	because I	could	study.
couldn't		couldn't	
had to		had to	

D. Fill in the blanks.

1. Bill _____ able to go to the beach yesterday because it was raining.

2. I'm glad you _____ able to help me with my science project next weekend.

3. Sally and Jane _____ able to walk home from the party because it was too dark.

4. I couldn't pay my rent last month, but

   I'm sure _____ able to pay it next month.

5. I'm sorry I _____ able to arrive on time yesterday afternoon.

   I _____ fix a flat tire.

6. If you want to put your hair in a ponytail,

   _____ got to have long hair.

7. My daughter _____ able to go to school next week because

   _____ got to have an operation.

E. Listen to the story, and then choose the correct answers to the questions you hear.

Poor Janet!

1. a. She could dance in the school play.
   b. She wasn't able to dance in the school play.

2. a. She practiced every day.
   b. She didn't practice.

3. a. She fell down and cut herself.
   b. She fell down and hurt herself.

4. a. She'll be able to dance in the play.
   b. She can't dance in the play this year.

FAMILIES AND TIME

Read the article on student book page 103 and answer the questions.

1. According to this article, people today are spending less time _____.
   a. at work
   b. alone
   c. with their friends
   d. on the Internet

2. In the past in many countries, the mother didn't _____.
   a. shop
   b. take care of the children
   c. stay home
   d. go to work

3. This article talks about technology _____.
   a. for transportation
   b. for housework
   c. for communication
   d. for medicine

4. In paragraph 3, *many children come home from school to an empty apartment* means _____.
   a. there isn't any furniture in the apartment
   b. there aren't any adults at home
   c. the refrigerator is empty
   d. there aren't any toys for the children to play with

5. According to the article, in a single-parent family, _____.
   a. the single parent is very busy
   b. the single parent stays home
   c. there is only one child
   d. both parents work

6. According to this article, technology _____.
   a. brings families closer together
   b. can make it difficult for families to communicate with each other
   c. is always bad
   d. is a problem for people who are far away

7. The main idea of paragraph 2 is _____.
   a. fathers work
   b. single parents have to do everything
   c. there are many single parents
   d. parents today don't have as much time for their children as in the past

8. An activity that this article does NOT talk about is _____.
   a. watching TV
   b. using the Internet
   c. listening to music
   d. talking on the phone

SIDE by SIDE Gazette

STUDENT BOOK PAGES **103–104**

B **FAMILIES AND TIME: Life in Your Home**

Answer these questions about yourself.

1. Who lives with you? Who are the people in your home?

   ....

2. Who does the cooking? .... Who does the cleaning? ....

   Who does the food shopping? .... Who fixes things? ....

3. What things does your family do together?

   ....

4. How many hours a week do you . . .

   watch TV? .... use a computer? .... use a cell phone or smartphone? ....

C BUILD YOUR VOCABULARY! Mixed-Up Words

Unscramble the letters and write the home appliance words.

1. reryd _____

2. startoe _____

3. noir _____

4. wishredash _____

5. vimeworca _____

6. baggare soapslid _____

7. effcoe kream _____

8. ginsawh camineh _____

D BUILD YOUR VOCABULARY! Categories

Write the words from Exercise C in the correct categories.

Appliances for Clothing Care

_____

_____

_____

Appliances for Food Preparation

_____

_____

_____

Appliances for Food Cleanup

_____

_____

E BUILD YOUR VOCABULARY! What's the Word?

Write the correct word from Exercise C to complete each sentence.

1. After you wash the clothes, put them in the _____.

2. You can throw that old food in the sink. We have a _____.

3. It'll take only five minutes to cook those vegetables in the _____.

4. The _____ is broken. You'll have to wash those glasses in the sink.

5. Can I put this blouse in the _____, or should I wash it by hand?

6. I can't wear this shirt. It looks terrible. I need the _____.

7. We don't have a _____, so we'll have to eat our jam on cold bread.

8. Put four cups of water in the _____.

Look at the Fact File on student book page 103 and answer the questions.

1. The average person in France works _____ hours per year.
   a. one thousand five hundred sixty
   b. one thousand six hundred fifty-six
   c. one thousand nine hundred sixty-six
   d. one thousand eight-hundred ninety-nine

2. The average person in the United States doesn't work as many hours as the average person in _____.
   a. France
   b. Japan
   c. Germany
   d. Thailand

3. The average person in _____ works 310 more hours per year than the average person in France.
   a. Thailand
   b. the United States
   c. Japan
   d. Germany

4. The average person in Thailand works 311 more hours per year than the average person in _____.
   a. the United States
   b. France
   c. Japan
   d. Germany

5. The average person in France works _____ per year than the average person in Germany.
   a. 96 more hours
   b. 4 more hours
   c. 104 more hours
   d. 116 more hours

6. The country where people spend the most time at work is in _____.
   a. North America
   b. South America
   c. Europe
   d. Asia

7. If the average person in Thailand works 50 weeks a year, he or she works _____.
   a. forty hours per week
   b. forty-two hours per week
   c. forty-four hours per week
   d. forty-five hours per week

8. If the average person in the United States works 50 weeks a year, he or she works almost _____.
   a. 45 hours a week
   b. 40 hours a week
   c. 35 hours a week
   d. 30 hours a week

G "CAN-DO" REVIEW

Match the "can do" statement and the correct sentence.

_____ 1. I can express concern about someone.

_____ 2. I can react to information with surprise.

_____ 3. I can apologize.

_____ 4. I can admit a mistake.

_____ 5. I can express sympathy.

_____ 6. I can express past inability.

_____ 7. I can express future inability.

_____ 8. I can describe my emotions.

_____ 9. I can describe another person's emotions.

_____ 10. I can express obligation.

a. I'm sorry to hear that.

b. I couldn't finish my homework.

c. He's angry.

d. Really?

e. I won't be able to work tomorrow.

f. I have to take my dog to the vet.

g. You look upset.

h. I'm sorry.

i. I guess I made a mistake.

j. I'm upset.

A MATCHING

You're going for a checkup tomorrow. What will happen?

_d_ 1. The nurse will lead you   **a.** a chest X-ray.

____ 2. You'll stand   **b.** your heart with a stethoscope.

____ 3. The nurse will measure   **c.** about your health.

____ 4. A lab technician will do   **d.** into an examination room.

____ 5. An X-ray technician will take   **e.** your height and weight.

____ 6. The doctor will listen to   **f.** a cardiogram.

____ 7. The doctor will do   **g.** on a scale.

____ 8. The doctor will talk to you   **h.** some blood tests.

B HOW WAS YOUR MEDICAL CHECKUP?

1. I had a complete _____.
   a. health
   (b.) examination

2. First, the nurse led me into _____.
   a. a test
   b. an examination room

3. I _____ on a scale.
   a. stood
   b. examined

4. The nurse measured my _____.
   a. heart
   b. height

5. Then she _____ my blood pressure.
   a. took
   b. did

6. The lab technician did some _____.
   a. blood tests
   b. blood pressure

7. The doctor _____ my hand.
   a. look
   b. shook

8. He _____ my throat.
   a. listened
   b. examined

9. He did a _____.
   a. cardiogram
   b. stethoscope

10. He talked with me about my _____.
    a. healthy
    b. health

C WENDY IS WORRIED ABOUT HER HEALTH

less	fewer	more

Wendy is worried about her health. She always feels tired, and she doesn't know why. In January, Wendy went to see Dr. Jansen. Dr. Jansen thinks Wendy feels tired because she eats too much sugar. According to Dr. Jansen, Wendy must eat (–) __fewer__[1] cookies and (–) _____[2] ice cream.

Also, Wendy must eat (+) _____[3] green vegetables and (+) _____[4] nuts. Wendy tried Dr. Jansen's diet, but it didn't help.

In March, Wendy went to see Dr. Martin. Dr. Martin thinks Wendy feels tired because she's too thin. According to Dr. Martin, Wendy must eat (–) _____[5] vegetables and (–) _____[6] lean meat. Also, Wendy must eat (+) _____[7] candy and (+) _____[8] potatoes. Wendy tried Dr. Martin's diet, but it didn't help.

In April, Wendy went to see Dr. Appleton. Dr. Appleton thinks Wendy feels tired because she eats too much spicy food. According to Dr. Appleton, Wendy must eat (–) _____[9] pepper and (–) _____[10] onions. Also, Wendy must drink (+) _____[11] skim milk and (+) _____[12] water. Wendy tried Dr. Appleton's diet, but it didn't help.

In May, Wendy went to see Dr. Mayfield. Dr. Mayfield thinks Wendy feels tired because she eats too much salt. According to Dr. Mayfield, Wendy must eat (–) _____[13] french fries and (–) _____[14] salt. Also, Wendy must eat (+) _____[15] yogurt and (+) _____[16] fish. Wendy tried Dr. Mayfield's diet, but it didn't help.

Now Wendy needs YOUR help. What do you think?

Wendy must eat/drink (–) ....

Also, she must eat/drink (+) ....

Listen. Then clap and practice.

Candy,   cookies,   ice cream,   cake!

Candy,   cookies,   ice cream,   cake!

Eat less   candy!

Fewer   cookies!

Eat less   ice cream!

Eat less   cake!

Candy,   cookies,   ice cream,   cake!

Candy,   cookies,   ice cream,   cake!

Carrots,   beans,   grapefruit, greens!

Carrots,   beans,   grapefruit, greens!

Eat more   carrots!

Eat more   beans!

Eat more   grapefruit!

Eat more   greens!

Carrots,   beans,   grapefruit, greens!

Carrots,   beans,   grapefruit, greens!

| must | | answer | dress | repair | type |

1. Here at the Greenly Company, you

   ___must dress___ neatly, and

   you ___must type___ accurately.

2. Remember, you _____ the

   telephone politely, and you _____

   _____ the cars carefully.

| must | | arrive | file | sort | work |

3. Here at the Tip Top Company, every

   employee _____ on time

   and _____ hard.

4. It's very important. You _____

   the mail carefully, and you _____

   _____ accurately.

| must | | cook | dance | sing | speak |

5. Remember, Ginger, you _____

   gracefully, and you _____

   beautifully.

6. Here at Joe's Diner, you _____

   the food quickly, and you _____

   _____ to the customers politely.

mustn't	don't have to	doesn't have to

1. You _____mustn't_____ arrive late for work.

2. Helen's doctor is concerned. He says she _____ eat too much candy.

3. According to my doctor, I _____ stop jogging, but I _____ jog so often.

4. Tomorrow is a holiday. The store is closed. The employees _____ work.

5. It's early. You _____ leave right now. But remember, you _____ leave too late.

6. My landlord is upset. He says I _____ play music after midnight.

7. Charlie is lucky. He _____ call the plumber because he was able to fix the sink by himself.

G THE BUTLER SCHOOL

must	mustn't	don't have to

At the Butler School you _____must_____ ¹ get to school on time

every morning. If you're late, your parents _____ ² write a note.

If you're sick, your parents _____ ³ call the school.

You can bring your lunch if you want to, but you

_____ ⁴ because we have a very nice cafeteria.

The boys _____ ⁵ always wear jackets, but if they don't want to wear ties, they

_____ ⁶. The girls _____ ⁷ wear dresses or skirts. Some girls want to wear

pants to school, but at the Butler School they _____ ⁸. Everyone _____ ⁹

have a notebook for every subject, and you _____ ¹⁰ forget to take your notebooks to

class. You can talk to your friends while you're working, but you _____ ¹¹ talk too

loudly. You _____ ¹² speak politely to your teacher, but you _____ ¹³ agree

with your teacher all the time. If you have a different opinion, your teacher will be happy to

listen. Finally, you _____ ¹⁴ always do your homework.

WRITE ABOUT YOUR SCHOOL

At our school, you must ....

You mustn't ....

You don't have to ....

I **YOU DECIDE:** *What Did They Say?*

must	mustn't

1. My parents told me ....

.... because I have a big test tomorrow.

2. Sally talked to her English teacher, and he told her ....

.... because she makes too many mistakes.

3. Robert talked to his girlfriend and she told him ....

.... because he works too much.

4. Grandpa talked to his doctor and she told him ....

.... because he's a little too heavy.

5. We talked to our landlord and he told us ....

.... because the neighbors are upset.

6. I talked to my grandmother and she told me ....

.... because life is short.

LISTENING

Listen and choose the correct answer.

1. a. You should watch TV more often.
   b. You must stop watching TV so often.

2. a. You must lose some weight.
   b. You should start eating rich desserts.

3. a. I should stop eating spicy foods.
   b. I must start eating spicy foods.

4. a. You must stop relaxing.
   b. You must take life a little easier.

5. a. You must start listening to loud music.
   b. You should stop listening to loud music.

6. a. I must stop jogging.
   b. I should jog more often.

K **GrammarRap:** *You Mustn't Eat Cookies*

Listen. Then clap and practice.

A. You mustn't eat   cookies.

B. You mustn't eat   cake.

C. You mustn't eat   butter.

D. You mustn't eat   steak.

A. You must eat   fruit.

B. You must eat   potatoes.

C. You must eat   fish.

D. You must eat   tomatoes.

L **GrammarRap:** *You Must . . .*

Listen. Then clap and practice.

A. You must clean your   room.

B. But I cleaned it on   Sunday!

A. You must do the   laundry.

B. But I did it last   Monday!

A. You must fix the   fence.

B. But I fixed it in   June!

A. You must do your   homework!

B. I'll finish it   soon!

LOUD AND CLEAR h!

Fill in the words. Then read the sentences aloud.

hotel	Hawaii	happy	here
Hi		Honolulu	

1. ___Hi___! We're ___happy___ we're

___here___ in our ___hotel___ in

___Honolulu___, ___Hawaii___!

history	Howard	half	hand
	have	homework	

2. Hurry, _____! You _____ to

_____ in your _____

_____ in _____ an hour.

hurt	Harry	helmet	his
	head	have	

3. Poor _____! He _____

_____ _____ because he

didn't _____ a _____.

hot dogs	Henry	has	heavy
	height	having	

4. _____ is too _____ for his

_____. He _____ to stop

_____ _____.

husband	has	healthy	he
	heart	Hilda's	

5. _____ _____ isn't

_____. _____ _____ problems

with his hearing and his _____.

hiccups	Hillary	headache
horrible	happy	has

6. _____ isn't _____.

She _____ the _____

and a _____ _____.

| bathe | exercise | iron | knit | mop | pay | rearrange | sew |

STUDENT BOOK
PAGES 115–124

1. Will Michael be busy this morning?

___Yes, he will___. ___He'll be mopping___
his floors.

2. Will your children be busy this afternoon?

_____. _____
the dog.

3. Will you and George be busy today?

_____. _____
at the health club.

4. Will Mr. and Mrs. Benson be busy today?

_____. _____
bills.

5. Will Kate be busy tomorrow afternoon?

_____. _____
a sweater.

6. Will you be busy this afternoon?

_____. _____
clothes.

7. Will Fred be busy this Saturday?

_____. _____
shirts.

8. Will you and your wife be busy tomorrow?

_____. _____
furniture.

Arthur was upset after he talked to Gloria. He decided to call Jennifer.

Hi, Jennifer. This is Arthur. Can I come over this afternoon?

No, Arthur. I'm afraid I won't be home this afternoon. I'll be _____

I see. Can I come over TOMORROW afternoon?

No, Arthur. I'm afraid I won't be home tomorrow afternoon. I'll be _____

Can I come over and visit this WEEKEND?

No, Arthur. I'll be _____

Well, can I come over and visit next Monday?

No, Arthur. I'll be _____

How about some time next AUTUMN?

No, Arthur. I'm getting married next autumn.

Oh, no! Not again!!

C. GRAMMARRAP: *What Do You Think?*

Listen. Then clap and practice.

A. What do you   think you'll be   doing next   spring?

B. I'll probably be   doing the   same old   thing.

A. What do you   think he'll be   doing this   fall?

B. I'm sure he'll be   working   downtown at the   mall.

A. When do you   think they'll be   leaving for   Spain?

B. I think they'll be   taking the   four o'clock   plane.

A. When do you   think you'll be   hearing from   Anne?

B. I'm sure she'll be   calling as   soon as she   can.

A. When do you   think we'll be   hearing from   Jack?

B. I'm sure he'll be   phoning as   soon as he's   back.

A. What do you   think she'll be   doing at   two?

B. I think she'll be   taking the   kids to the   zoo.

A. Where do you   think they'll be   living next   year?

B. As far as we   know, they'll be   living right   here.

bake	clean his apartment	exercise	study	wash her car
bathe their dog	do their laundry	practice the violin	take a bath	watch TV

1. A. Why don't you call Jane this Saturday?
   B. I don't want to disturb her. I'm sure

   _____ she'll be practicing the violin _____.

   She always _____ practices the violin _____
   on Saturday.

2. A. Why don't you call Carlos after dinner?
   B. I don't want to disturb him. I'm sure

   _____.

   He always _____
   after dinner.

3. A. Why don't you call Peggy and Bob tonight?
   B. I don't want to disturb them. I'm sure

   _____.

   They always _____
   on Monday night.

4. A. Why don't you call Nancy this afternoon?
   B. I don't want to disturb her. I'm sure

   _____.

   She usually _____
   in the afternoon.

5. A. Why don't you call your cousin Henry this morning?
   B. I don't want to disturb him. I'm sure

   _____.

   He always _____
   on Sunday morning.

6. A. Why don't you call Tom and Carol this evening?
   B. I don't want to disturb them. I'm sure

   _____.

   They always _____
   in the evening.

7. A. Why don't you call Elizabeth this this afternoon?

B. I don't want to disturb her. I'm sure

_____.

She usually _____
on Sunday afternoon.

8. A. Why don't you call your aunt and uncle this morning?

B. I don't want to disturb them. I'm sure

_____.

They always _____
on Saturday morning.

9. A. Why don't you call your friend George tonight?

B. I don't want to disturb him. I'm sure

_____.

He always _____
before he goes to bed.

10. A. Why don't you call Betty and Ben tonight?

B. I don't want to disturb them. I'm sure

_____.

They always _____
on Tuesday night.

 **LISTENING** 🔊

Listen and choose the correct answer.

1. a. buying dresses
  (b.) ironing dresses

2. a. working downtown
  b. walking downtown

3. a. sitting on the front porch
  b. knitting on the front porch

4. a. watching sports
  b. washing shorts

5. a. feeding the baby
  b. reading to the baby

6. a. taking a bus
  b. taking a bath

7. a. making pancakes
  b. baking cakes

8. a. doing her homework
  b. doing yoga

9. a. skiing
  b. sleeping

10. a. skateboarding
  b. skating

11. a. washing the dog
  b. walking the dog

12. a. singing about you
  b. thinking about you

called	isn't	message	right	take	that
hello	may	okay	speak	tell	this

A. ____Hello____ **1**.

B. Hello. _____ **2** is Brian. _____ **3** I please

_____ **4** to Cathy?

A. I'm sorry. Cathy _____ **5** here _____ **6** now.

Can I _____ **7** a _____ **8**?

B. Yes. Please _____ **9** Cathy _____ **10**

Brian _____ **11**.

A. _____ **12**.

B. Thank you.

Choose the correct response.

1. May I please speak to Ronald?
   a. Thank you.
   (b) Yes. Hold on a moment.

2. When can you come over?
   a. At three this afternoon.
   b. Don't worry.

3. I don't want to disturb you.
   a. Yes, I will.
   b. Don't worry. You won't disturb me.

4. We won't be able to come over and visit you tomorrow night.
   a. Oh. Why not?
   b. When?

5. I can come over tonight. Is that okay?
   a. I'll be glad.
   b. Sure. I'll see you then.

6. Sorry. I'll be eating dinner at seven.
   a. I don't want to disturb you.
   b. I'll disturb you.

7. Hello.
   a. Okay.
   b. Hello. This is Mrs. Miller.

8. Hi, Barbara. What's up?
   a. Fine.
   b. I'm having a test tomorrow.

9. I'm afraid I won't be home at three.
   a. Okay. I'll see you at three.
   b. Oh. How about six?

10. I'm having some problems with the homework for tomorrow.
   a. I'll be glad to help.
   b. I'm glad.

11. Will you be home this Wednesday afternoon?
   a. Yes. I'll be shopping.
   b. Yes. I'll be ironing.

12. How about nine o'clock?
   a. Fine. I'll see you then.
   b. Yes, it will.

at	for	in	until

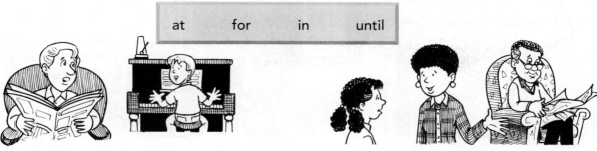

1. A. How much longer will you be practicing the piano?

B. ____I'll __be practicing____ the piano

____for____ another half hour.

2. A. How long will Grandpa be reading the newspaper?

B. _____ the newspaper

_____ he falls asleep.

3. A. How late will Jane be working at the office this evening?

B. _____ at the office

_____ ten o'clock.

4. A. Excuse me. When will we be arriving in San Francisco?

B. _____ in San Francisco

_____ six thirty.

5. A. When will you be having your yearly checkup?

B. _____ my yearly

checkup_____ a few weeks.

6. A. How late will Maria be studying English?

B. _____ English

_____ 8:30.

7. A. How long will your Uncle Willy be staying with us?

B. _____ with us

_____ next month.

8. A. How much longer will you be cooking on the barbecue?

B. _____ on the barbecue

_____ another ten minutes.

WHAT'S THE QUESTION?

1. How much longer <u>will you be talking on the telephone</u> ?

I'll be talking on the telephone for another half hour.

2. A. How late _____?

   B. They'll be arriving at midnight.

3. A. How long _____?

   B. She'll be working on his car all morning.

4. A. When _____?

   B. He'll be leaving in a little while.

5. A. How far _____?

   B. We'll be driving until we get to Miami.

6. A. How long _____?

   B. I'll be mopping the floors all morning.

7. A. How soon _____?

   B. She'll be feeding the dog when she gets home.

8. A. How much longer _____?

   B. They'll be living away from home until they finish college.

9. A. How late _____?

   B. He'll be playing loud music until 2 A.M.

10. How much longer _____?

We'll be riding on the roller-coaster for another five minutes.

Listen. Then clap and practice.

A.   How much   longer will you be   talking on the   phone?

B.   I'll be talking for a   few more   minutes.

A.   For a few more   minutes?

B.   That's what I   said.

  I'll be talking for a   few more   minutes.

A.   How much   longer will he be   working   at the mall?

B.   He'll be working for a   few more   hours.

A.   For a few more   hours?

B.   That's what he   said.

  He'll be working for a   few more   hours.

A.   How much   longer will she be staying in   Rome?

B.   She'll be staying for a   few more   days.

A.   For a few more   days?

B.   That's what she   said.

  She'll be staying for a   few more   days.

me	him	her	us	you	them
my	his	her	our	your	their
myself	himself	herself	ourselves	yourself	themselves
				yourselves	

STUDENT BOOK
PAGES **125–136**

13

1. _____His_____ family didn't help

   ____him____. He painted the fence

   by _____himself_____.

2. _____ parents didn't help

   _____. They made breakfast

   by _____.

3. _____ mother usually helps

   _____ put her hair in a ponytail.

   But today she did it by _____.

4. Do you need any help? I'll help _____.

   _____ don't have to rake the leaves

   by _____.

5. Nobody is helping _____.

   He's washing the dishes by _____.

6. I planted these flowers by _____.

   Nobody helped _____.

7. _____ teacher can't help

   _____. We've got to do our

   homework by _____.

8. You don't have to go on the roller-coaster

   by _____. I'll go with

   _____.

B THE LOST ROLLERBLADES

mine	his	hers	ours	yours	theirs

A. I just found these rollerblades. Are they _____yours_____ **1**?

B. No. They aren't _____ **2**. But they might be Jim's. He always forgets things.

A. No. I don't think they're _____ **3**. His rollerblades are green, and these are black.

B. Do you think they might be Ms. Johnson's?

A. Our English teacher's?! No. They can't be _____ **4**. She doesn't have rollerblades.

B. How about Carol and Ted? Do you think these rollerblades might

be _____ **5**?

A. No, I don't think so. They never go rollerblading. I have an idea. Let's put the rollerblades in the school office.

B. Okay. And if nobody asks for them soon, I guess they'll be _____ **6**.

C SCRAMBLED SENTENCES

Unscramble the sentences.

1. his   he   by   fix   himself?   Did   car

   _____Did he fix his car by himself?_____

2. book   Is   yours?   address   this

   _____

3. cats   feed   by   She   can   the   herself.

   _____

4. you   number?   Did   her   him   telephone   give

   _____

5. Bob,   I   new   When   him   you   tell   call   his   sunglasses.   have

   _____

6. lost   because   to   cell   your   I   mine.   need   use   phone   I

   _____

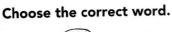

D WHAT'S THE WORD?

Choose the correct word.

1. I like to eat the _____ stew.
   (a.) chef's
   b. chefs'

2. I love my _____ birthday presents!
   a. grandmother's
   b. grandmothers'

3. Where's the _____ food?
   a. cat's
   b. cats'

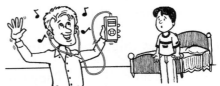

4. Do you listen to your _____ music?
   a. sons'
   b. son's

5. These are probably a _____ headphones.
   a. student's
   b. students'

6. Is this your _____ ring?
   a. girlfriends'
   b. girlfriend's

7. My _____ new painting is very ugly.
   a. cousin's
   b. cousins'

8. My _____ dog usually barks all night.
   a. neighbor's
   b. neighbors'

E LISTENING

Listen to each conversation, and then choose the correct answers to the questions you hear.

CONVERSATION 1

1. a. On the floor.
   (b.) On the desk.
   c. On the chair.

2. a. No, it isn't his.
   b. It might be his.
   c. Yes, it's his.

3. a. Last Tuesday.
   b. Last Monday.
   c. Last Thursday.

CONVERSATION 2

4. a. Black.
   b. Brown.
   c. Blue.

5. a. Her watch.
   b. Her umbrella.
   c. Her wallet.

6. a. Yes, it's hers.
   b. No, it isn't hers.
   c. It might be hers.

NOISY NEIGHBORS!

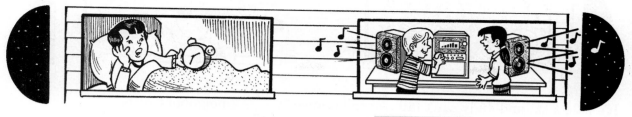

It's 1:30 A.M., and James can't fall asleep because his [neighbors / (neighbors')]¹ children

[are listening / will be listening]² to loud music. Last night they [listened / listening]³ to loud music [until / for]⁴

four hours, and James [couldn't / wasn't]⁵ able to [fall / fell]⁶ asleep. He's very worried because he

studies [hardly / hard]⁷ every day, and he needs to sleep [at / in the]⁸ night. Tomorrow he thinks

[he'll call / he calls]⁹ [him / his]¹⁰ landlord.

It's 2 A.M., and I'm not asleep because my [next-door / downstairs]¹¹ neighbors are rearranging

[there / their]¹² furniture. They're very [noisily / noisy]¹³! I don't like [complain / to complain]¹⁴, but if they

[move / will move]¹⁵ furniture again tomorrow night, I'll talk [to / at]¹⁶ the landlord, or I'll call them

[themselves / myself]¹⁷.

(continued)

Activity Workbook 123

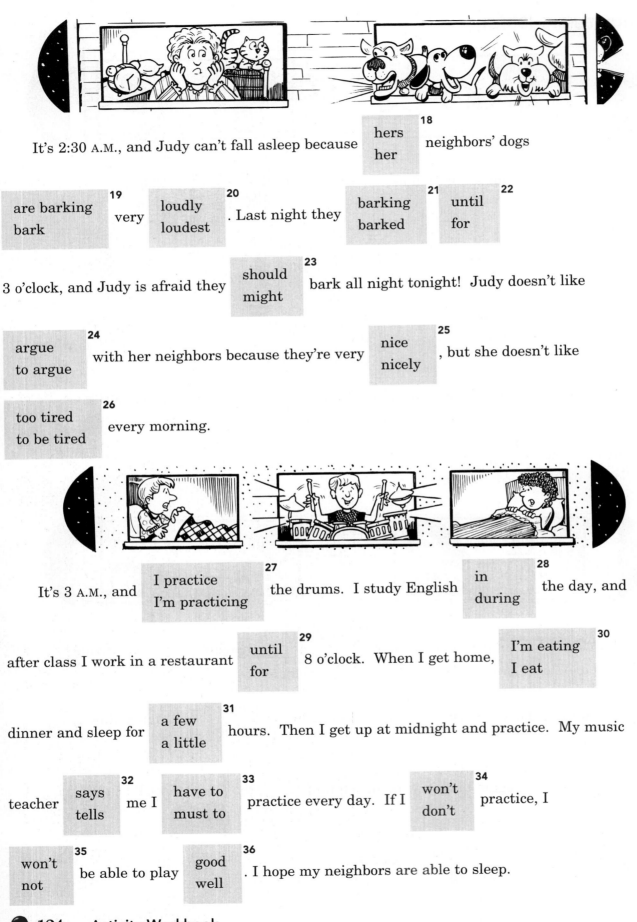

It's 2:30 A.M., and Judy can't fall asleep because [hers / her]¹⁸ neighbors' dogs

[are barking / bark]¹⁹ very [loudly / loudest]²⁰. Last night they [barking / barked]²¹ [until / for]²²

3 o'clock, and Judy is afraid they [should / might]²³ bark all night tonight! Judy doesn't like

[argue / to argue]²⁴ with her neighbors because they're very [nice / nicely]²⁵, but she doesn't like

[too tired / to be tired]²⁶ every morning.

It's 3 A.M., and [I practice / I'm practicing]²⁷ the drums. I study English [in / during]²⁸ the day, and

after class I work in a restaurant [until / for]²⁹ 8 o'clock. When I get home, [I'm eating / I eat]³⁰

dinner and sleep for [a few / a little]³¹ hours. Then I get up at midnight and practice. My music

teacher [says / tells]³² me I [have to / must to]³³ practice every day. If I [won't / don't]³⁴ practice, I

[won't / not]³⁵ be able to play [good / well]³⁶. I hope my neighbors are able to sleep.

1. A. I don't like Stuart. He never says [anyone / anything] nice.

   B. To tell the truth, [nobody / anybody] likes Stuart. He never says [anything / something] nice about [nobody / anybody]!

2. A. I can't fix my video camera. Is there [anyone / anything] you can do to help?

   B. No. I'm afraid [nobody / somebody] here can help you.

   You'll have to fix it by [himself / yourself].

3. A. Look! [Anybody / Somebody] ate all the cake!

   B. That's terrible! [Anybody / Nobody] will be able to have it for dessert tonight!

4. A. There's [anyone / someone] on the phone for you.

   B. Who is it?

   A. I don't have [any / some] idea.

(continued)

5. A. I can't hook up my new printer. Does [anybody / nobody] here know how to do it?

B. You should ask the supervisor. She knows [anyone / someone] who can do it.

6. A. How was the party last night?

B. It was terrible! I didn't know [anyone / somebody] there,

and [anybody / nobody] talked to me.

7. A. What's that noise? I think [anybody / somebody] is in the basement!

B. I don't hear [nothing / anything]. Don't worry. [Nobody / Anybody]

is in the basement.

A. Are you sure? I definitely hear [anything / something].

B. Don't worry. [Nobody / Anybody] is there.

H **LISTENING: The Prom**

Listen and choose the correct response.

1. a. No, I wasn't.
    (b.) I didn't enjoy myself very much.

2. a. It wasn't very comfortable.
    b. She was very talkative.

3. a. It was too crowded.
    b. It was too soft.

4. a. Until 10:30.
    b. In a few hours.

5. a. I missed the bus.
    b. I wasn't having a good time.

6. a. I'm sure it is.
    b. We'll just have to wait and see.

A. Hello. May I please speak to Maggie Winters?

B. ....

A. There's something wrong with my dishwasher, and I need a repairperson who can come over and fix it.

B. ....

A. No. There isn't any water on the kitchen floor, but the dishwasher won't turn on.

B. ....

A. I don't know. It worked yesterday, but it isn't working today.

B. ....

A. I live at 234 School Street in Westville.

B. ....

A. Drive down Center Street and turn right. My house is the last one on the left.

B. ....

A. I'm sorry. I'm afraid I won't be home at 9:00 tomorrow morning. Can you come at any other time?

B. ....

A. Can you come a little earlier?

B. ....

A. That's fine. I'll see you then. Good-bye.

B. Good-bye.

Listen. Then clap and practice.

A. Who cleans your house?

B. I clean it myself.

A. Does your wife help you?

B. She helps me if I ask her.

A. Who does your laundry?

B. I do it myself.

A. Does your husband help you?

B. He helps me if I ask him.

A. Who washes the dishes?

B. He washes them himself.

A. Does his daughter help him?

B. She helps him if he asks her.

A. Who makes breakfast?

B. She makes it herself.

A. Does her father help her?

B. He helps her if she asks him.

A. Who does your shopping?

B. We do it ourselves.

A. Do your children help you?

B. They help us if we ask them.

A. Who does their homework?

B. They do it themselves.

A. Does their mother help them?

B. She helps them if they ask her.

YOU DECIDE: *Why Can't They Go to the Baseball Game?*

A. Would you like to go to a baseball game with me on Saturday?

B. ....

A. That's too bad. Do you think your sister might be able to go?

B. ....

A. Oh, I forgot. She's busy every Saturday. How about your cousins? They like baseball.

B. ....

A. Oh. I hope they enjoy themselves. Do you think your father might want to go?

B. ....

A. That's too bad. Nobody told me. How did it happen?

B. ....

A. Well, I hope he's better soon. You know, I guess I'll go to work on Saturday.

B. ....

A. Really? Our boss likes baseball?!

B. ....

A. Okay. I'll call him and see if he wants to go with me. Good-bye.

B. ....

L **LISTENING**

Listen and choose the person you should call.

1. a. a plumber
   b. a mechanic
   c. a doctor

2. a. a lab technician
   b. an electrician
   c. a plumber

3. a. a doctor
   b. a locksmith
   c. a dentist

4. a. a mechanic
   b. a plumber
   c. the landlord

5. a. an electrician
   b. a plumber
   c. a painter

6. a. a mechanic
   b. the police
   c. a repairperson

7. a. a chef
   b. an electrician
   c. a plumber

8. a. a teacher
   b. a repairperson
   c. a mechanic

Circle the correct word.

1. ~~Too~~ **(Two)** cats are **(too)** ~~two~~ many cats for me!

2. Last weak / week I was too weak / week to get out of bed.

3. Their / They're going to go for their / they're annual physical examination.

4. You're right / write . I should right / write my term paper this weekend.

5. Wear / Where are my glasses? I need to wear / where them.

6. We have an our / hour to do our / hour exercises.

7. Do you no / know a good dentist? No, / Know, I don't.

8. You should by / buy a camera and take pictures of your children by / buy yourself.

9. There's a big hole / whole in my slice of hole / whole wheat bread!

10. You're / Your late. You're / Your guests arrived twenty minutes ago.

11. Yesterday they cooked ate / eight cakes for a party, and the guests ate / eight all the cakes.

Listen. Then clap and practice.

Does anybody   here speak   Spanish?

Does anybody   here speak   French?

Does anybody   here have a   hammer?

Does anyone   here have a   wrench?

Somebody   here speaks   Spanish.

Somebody   here speaks   French.

Somebody   here has a   hammer.

Someone   here has a   wrench.

Does anybody   here have   change for a   dollar?

Does anyone   here have   a dime?

Does anybody   here have a   map of the   city?

Does anyone   here have the   time?

Nobody   here has   change for a   dollar.

Nobody   here has   a dime.

Nobody   here has a   map of the   city.

Nobody   here has the   time.

✓ CHECK-UP TEST: Chapters 11–13

A. Complete the sentences.

Ex. Will you be home this evening?
Yes, I will. (knit)

_____ I'll **be knitting** _____.

1. Will your parents be busy today?
Yes, they will. (pay)

_____ bills.

2. Will you be leaving home soon?
Yes, I will. (go)

_____ to college.

3. Will your brother be home at 5:00?
Yes, he will. (read)

_____ his e-mail.

4. Will Karen be at the office tonight?
Yes, she will. (work)

_____ until 9:00.

5. Will you and your girlfriend be busy this Saturday?
Yes, we will. (get married)

_____.

B. Complete the sentences.

Ex. When _____ **will you be visiting us** _____?
We'll be visiting you next January.

1. How late _____

_____?
I'll be practicing the piano until 8:00.

2. How much longer _____

_____?
He'll be ironing for a few more minutes.

3. How soon _____

_____?
She'll be leaving in a little while.

4. How far _____

_____?
They'll be driving until they get to Denver.

5. How long _____

_____?
We'll be chatting online for a few hours.

C. Circle the correct answers.

1. My doctor says I must eat [less / fewer] ice cream,

[less / fewer] french fries, and [less / fewer] fatty meat.

2. I [mustn't / don't have to] solve this math problem

tonight, but I want to.

3. Jim [mustn't / doesn't have to] eat too [much / many]

spicy food because he has stomach problems.

4. If you want to get a job in this office, you must speak English and Spanish, but you

[mustn't / don't have to] type very fast.

5. My son will be performing in the school

play [for / until] a week.

6. She'll be staying in Chicago [for / until] Friday.

7. They finished at / in 8:00.

8. I'll be arriving at / in noon.

9. I need anyone / someone who can fix my

camcorder. I don't know anything / something

about camcorders.

10. If you look in the phone book, I'm sure you'll

find anybody / somebody who can fix your VCR.

11. Anyone / Someone borrowed my mop, and now

I can't clean the floors.

12. This is his car. It isn't my / mine .

13. I don't think this is their / theirs cell phone,

but it might be her / hers .

14. We gave her / his our headphones.

15. This camera isn't ours / our .

D. Listen and choose the correct answers to complete the sentences.

1. a. a complete physical examination.
b. an examination room.

2. a. your blood.
b. your height and your weight.

3. a. blood pressure.
b. stethoscope.

4. a. a pulse.
b. an X-ray.

5. a. eyes, ears, nose, and throat.
b. checkup.

A COMMUNITIES

Read the article on student book page 137 and answer the questions.

1. In suburban communities, people usually live _____.
   a. far from a city
   b. in apartment buildings
   c. in separate houses
   d. on busy streets

2. In rural communities, people live _____.
   a. near public transportation
   b. in apartment buildings
   c. in neighborhoods
   d. far from their neighbors

3. In urban communities, people DON'T live _____.
   a. close together
   b. in neighborhoods
   c. in the countryside
   d. in small houses

4. If you live in a rural area, the best way to get places is to _____.
   a. walk
   b. drive
   c. take the bus
   d. take the train

5. In the past, most people lived in _____.
   a. urban communities
   b. megacities
   c. suburban communities
   d. rural areas

6. According to the experts, in the future people will live in _____.
   a. very large suburban communities
   b. very large urban communities
   c. very large rural communities
   d. cities with one or two million people

7. *People keep to themselves* in paragraph 5 means _____.
   a. they aren't friendly with their neighbors
   b. they're dishonest
   c. they spend very little money
   d. they work hard

8. *Time will tell* in the last paragraph means _____.
   a. future communities will be friendly
   b. future communities won't be friendly
   c. we'll just have to wait and see if future communities are friendly
   d. we'll just have to wait and see if the experts are right

SIDE by SIDE Gazette

STUDENT BOOK
PAGES **137–138**

B COMMUNITIES: Describe Your Community

Answer these questions about the place where you live. (You can write short answers here, or write a composition about your community on a separate sheet of paper.)

Is your community urban, suburban, or rural? ....

What stores and businesses are near where you live? ....

Describe public transportation. How do you get to places? ....

Do you know your neighbors? Who are they? ....

Do children in the neighborhood play together? If yes, where? ....

Do you like your community? Why, or why not? ....

C BUILD YOUR VOCABULARY! What's the Word?

Choose the correct word.

1. Alexander is afraid to light a fire in his fireplace. He's going to call

an appliance repairperson
a chimneysweep

2. Carol's TV is broken. She's calling a

TV repairperson
cable TV installer

3. Ed has mice in his basement. He's calling

an exterminator
a chimneysweep

4. The Smith family wants to get more TV channels. The cable TV company will

   send | a TV repairperson | to their
   |---|
   | an installer |

   apartment.

5. Jennifer's dishwasher is making terrible noises. She's going to call an

exterminator
appliance repairperson

D BUILD YOUR VOCABULARY! Crossword

Across

5. If your TV isn't working, call a TV _____.

6. If the outside of your house looks old and dirty, call a house _____.

Down

1. If you want cable TV, call a cable TV _____.

2. If your chimney is dirty, call a _____.

3. If there are cockroaches in your apartment, call an _____.

4. If your refrigerator is broken, call an _____ repairperson.

E FACT FILE

Look at the Fact File on student book page 137 and answer the questions.

1. In 2010 the largest city in the world had about _____ people.
   a. 25 million
   b. 20 million
   c. 27 million
   d. 29 million

2. In 2010 _____ had about 25 million people.
   a. Shanghai
   b. São Paulo
   c. Tokyo
   d. Lagos

3. _____ wasn't one of the world's 10 largest cities in 1950, but it was in 2010.
   a. Calcutta
   b. Tokyo
   c. Beijing
   d. Buenos Aires

4. In 1950 Shanghai and _____ had about the same number of people.
   a. Tokyo
   b. Moscow
   c. Lagos
   d. Calcutta

5. In 1950 the largest city in the world had about _____ people.
   a. 8 million
   b. 9 million
   c. 12 million
   d. 15 million

6. In 2010 New York had a larger population than _____.
   a. London
   b. Lagos
   c. Mumbai
   d. Mexico City

7. In 2010 _____ countries had more than 20 million people.
   a. four
   b. five
   c. six
   d. three

8. In 2010 Tokyo had about _____ more people than it did in 1950.
   a. 12 million
   b. 17 million
   c. 22 million
   d. 25 million

F "CAN-DO" REVIEW

Match the "can do" statement and the correct sentence.

____ 1. I can describe a medical problem.

____ 2. I can express concern.

____ 3. I can give advice.

____ 4. I can tell about future plans.

____ 5. I can express enthusiasm.

____ 6. I can leave a telephone message.

____ 7. I can express hopes.

____ 8. I can offer to help.

____ 9. I can ask for a recommendation.

____ 10. I can describe a housing problem.

a. I'll be cleaning my apartment this evening.

b. Do you know anybody who can help me?

c. Please tell Julia that Eva called.

d. I'll be happy to help you.

e. I'm worried about your weight.

f. My garbage disposal is broken.

g. I think you should start doing exercises.

h. I hope you sleep better tonight.

i. I have a headache.

j. That's great!

A DAYS, MONTHS, AND ABBREVIATIONS

Look at the abbreviations. Write the days and months.

1. WED   _Wednesday_
2. MON   _____
3. SAT   _____
4. TUE   _____
5. FRI   _____
6. THU   _____
7. SUN   _____
8. MAR   _____
9. OCT   _____
10. JAN   _____

11. MAY   _____
12. NOV   _____
13. FEB   _____
14. JUL   _____
15. AUG   _____
16. DEC   _____
17. JUN   _____
18. APR   _____
19. SEP   _____

B DATES

Write the dates in numbers.

1. January 8, 2017   _0 1_ / _0 8_ / _1 7_
2. July 10, 2018   — —/— —/— —
3. March 12, 2016   — —/— —/— —
4. May 3, 2014   — —/— —/— —
5. September 5, 2015   — —/— —/— —
6. November 30, 2020   — —/— —/— —

7. April 9, 2019   — —/— —/— —
8. February 22, 2017   — —/— —/— —
9. August 1, 1989   — —/— —/— —
10. October 2, 2016   — —/— —/— —
11. December 6, 2018   — —/— —/— —
12. June 4, 2005   — —/— —/— —

C A REGISTRATION FORM

Complete the form with your own information.

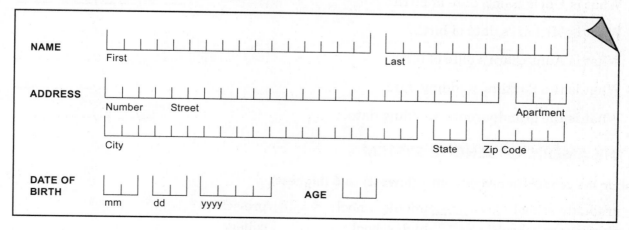

NUMERACY: A Calendar, Dates, and Ordinal Numbers

Look at the calendar. Write the correct dates.

November 2016						
Sunday	Monday	Tuesday	Wednesday	Thursday	Friday	Saturday
		1	2	3	4	5 Grandparents' 50th anniversary
6	7	8	9	10 Ana's 20th birthday!	11	12
13	14 Uncle Sam's 40th birthday!	15	16	17	18 Aunt Clara's 48th birthday!	19
20 Parkers' 25th anniversary	21	22	23 Michael's 12th birthday!	24	25	26
27	28	29	30			

1. What is the first Monday of the month?   Monday, November ____7____

2. What is the second Tuesday of the month?   Tuesday, November _____

3. What is the third Thursday of the month?   Thursday, November _____

4. What is the fifth Wednesday of the month?   Wednesday, November _____

5. What is Ana's date of birth? (month/day/year)   __ __/__ __/__ __ __ __

6. What is Uncle Sam's date of birth?   __ __/__ __/__ __ __ __

7. What is Michael's date of birth?   __ __/__ __/__ __ __ __

8. What is Aunt Clara's date of birth?   __ __/__ __/__ __ __ __

9. What is the Parkers' wedding date?   __ __/__ __/__ __ __ __

10. What is the grandparents' wedding date?   __ __/__ __/__ __ __ __

E **THE AMERICAN SCHOOL SYSTEM**

Number the schools in order from 1 (lowest) to 6 (highest).

____ graduate school   ____ middle school   __1__ pre-school

____ elementary school   ____ high school   ____ college

A) SCHOOL PERSONNEL

Match the school personnel with the work they do.

_g_ 1. The school nurse

2. The P.E. teacher

3. The librarian

4. The cafeteria workers

5. The security officer

6. The principal

7. The guidance counselor

a. makes sure the school is safe.

b. helps students choose their classes.

c. manages the whole school.

d. serve food to the students.

e. teaches physical education.

f. manages the library.

g. takes care of students when they feel sick.

B) A SCHOOL FLOOR PLAN

Look at the Milford Middle School Floor Plan. Decide if the sentences are True (T) or False (F).

Milford Middle School

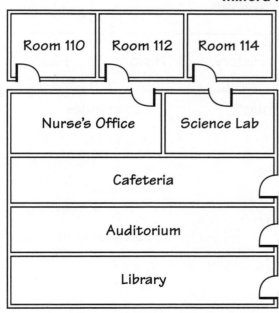

_T_ 1. The nurse's office is next to the science lab.

2. The gym is across from the nurse's office.

3. The P.E. teacher works in the room next to the science teacher.

4. Room 116 is across from the computer lab.

5. The librarian works across from the school secretary.

6. The cafeteria is across from the gym.

7. The art room is between the computer lab and Room 117.

8. Room 114 is across from the science lab.

9. The school office is next to the principal's office.

10. The library is between the auditorium and the cafeteria.

NUMERACY: Word Problems with Elapsed Time

Look at Laura's school schedule. Answer the questions.

	Monday	Tuesday	Wednesday	Thursday	Friday
Period 1 8:00 – 8:45	English	English	English	English	English
Period 2 9:00 – 9:45	Science	Science	Science	Science	Science
Period 3 10:00 – 10:45	Math	Math	Math	Math	Math
Period 4 11:00 – 11:45	Library	P.E.	Computer Lab	P.E.	Computer Lab
11:45 – 12:15	LUNCH	LUNCH	LUNCH	LUNCH	LUNCH
Period 5 12:15 – 1:00	Spanish	Spanish	Spanish	Spanish	Music
Period 6 1:15 – 2:00	History	History	History	History	History

1. How much time does Laura have for lunch every day?   _____ minutes

2. How long is Laura's school day?   _____ hours

3. How much time does Laura spend in Spanish class each week?   _____ hours

4. How much time does Laura spend in Science class each week?   _____ hours and _____ minutes

5. How much more time does Laura spend in History class than in Music class each week?   _____ hours

6. How much more time does Laura spend in the computer lab than in the library each week?   _____ minutes

7. How much more time does Laura spend in English class than in P.E. each week?   _____ hours and _____ minutes

D **PARTS OF A COMPUTER**

Unscramble the letters and write the names of the computer parts.

1. darkyobe   _____keyboard_____   4. owper lebca   _____

2. troinom   _____   5. worpe tubnot   _____

3. suemo   _____   6. bus torp   _____

A A SUPERMARKET RECEIPT

Look at the receipt. Answer the questions.

```
         Food Land

1 LB. @ $2.99 LB.
MUSHROOMS                 2.99

ICE CREAM 1 QT.           3.49

3 LBS. @ $1.50 LB
APPLES                    4.50

4 @ $.25
BANANAS                   1.00

3 LBS. @ $1.99 LB
CHICKEN                   5.97

MILK 1 GAL.               3.99

3 @ $1.00
SOUP                      3.00
..........................
            TOTAL    $24.94
            CASH     $25.00
            CHANGE     $.06
```

1. The person spent _____ on mushrooms.

2. A pound of chicken costs _____.

3. Three pounds of apples cost _____.

4. One banana costs _____.

5. Three cans of soup cost _____.

6. This person bought a _____ of milk and
    a _____ of ice cream.

7. This person spent _____ at the store.

B A FOOD LABEL

Read the food label. Answer the questions.

1. How much is one serving?
    a. one cup
    b. two cups
    c. a container

2. How many servings are in the
    container?
    a. one cup
    b. two cups
    c. one quart

```
Fruit Yogurt
Nutrition Facts
Serving Size 1 cup
Servings per Container  2
_____
Calories  240          Calories from Fat  25
                              % Daily Value
Total Fat  3 g                        4%
Cholesterol  15 mg                    5%
Sodium  140 mg                        6%
Total Carbohydrate  46 g             15%
_____
Vitamin A    10%    •    Vitamin C   4%
Calcium      35%    •    Iron        0%
         Keep Refrigerated
```

3. How many vitamins are in this yogurt?
    a. one
    b. two
    c. three

4. How much fat is in one serving of this yogurt?
    a. 25
    b. three milligrams
    c. three grams

5. How many calories are in each serving?
    a. 120
    b. 240
    c. 480

6. Where do you keep this yogurt?
    a. in the refrigerator
    b. in the freezer
    c. on the counter

C NUMERACY: Supermarket Math – Receipts

Look at the receipts. Answer the questions.

```
         Food World

2 LBS. @ $2.25/LB.
   MUSHROOMS              4.50

ICE CREAM                 3.75

MILK 1/2 GAL.             2.75

2 @ $1.75
   KETCHUP                3.50
..........................................
              TOTAL    $_____
              CASH     $ 20.00
              CHANGE   $_____
```

```
        Moon's Market

BAGGED CARROTS                1.75
GREEN BEANS
  2.5 LBS. @ $2.00/LB.        5.00
GRAPES
  2 LBS. @ $1.19/LB.          2.38
LETTUCE
  2 @ $1.75/HEAD              3.50
BANANAS
  3 LBS. @ $.50/LB.           1.50
..................................................
              TOTAL    $  14.13
              CASH     $  15.00
              CHANGE   $    .87
```

1. How much is the total?

_____

2. How much is the change?

_____

3. How much did he spend on fruit?

_____

4. How much did he spend on vegetables?

_____

D NUMERACY: Supermarket Math – Unit Pricing

Look at the supermarket advertisements. Check the store with the lower price.

GREEN'S GROCERIES

Crunch Breakfast Cereal
Buy one, get one free. (regular price $2.99)

Belle Farm Bread $3.00/loaf

Green's Orange Juice 1 quart
2 for $4.00

Granny's Chicken Soup
$1.50 a can

Simply Soda
4 cans for $1

~RAY'S~

Crunch Breakfast Cereal $1.99 each

Belle Farm Bread Buy 2, get one free.
 (regular price $3.50)

Orange Juice 1 quart $2.50

Ray's Chicken Soup 4 cans for $5

Drink Up Soda 40 cents a can

		Green's	Ray's			Green's	Rays
1.	One box of breakfast cereal	☐	✓	4.	One quart of orange juice	☐	☐
2.	Two boxes of breakfast cereal	☐	☐	5.	One can of grape soda	☐	☐
3.	Three loaves of Belle Farm Bread	☐	☐	6.	One can of chicken soup	☐	☐

E UNITS OF MEASURE & THEIR ABBREVIATIONS

Look at the chart. Write the words for these abbreviations.

Liquid Measures

3 teaspoons = 1 tablespoon	1 pint = 2 cups = 16 fluid ounces
2 tablespoons = 1 fluid ounce	1 quart = 2 pints = 32 fluid ounces
4 tablespoons = 1/4 cup	4 quarts = 1 gallon = 128 fluid ounces
1 cup = 8 fluid ounces	

Weights

4 ounces = 1/4 pound
8 ounces = 1/2 pound
16 ounces = one pound

1. fl. oz. _____fluid ounce_____

2. tsp. _____

3. c. _____

4. Tbsp. _____

5. gal. _____

6. qt. _____

7. pt. _____

8. lb. _____

F NUMERACY: Units of Measure

Look at the chart in Exercise E. Put these units of measure in order from the smallest (1) to the largest (7).

_____	one cup
_____	one tablespoon
_____	one fluid ounce
_____	one gallon
_____	one pint
___1___	one teaspoon
_____	one quart

G NUMERACY: Quantities in a Recipe

Look at the recipe on the left. Then complete the recipe on the right.

Party Punch
(makes 15 servings)

2 quarts orange juice

1 qt. lemon/lime soda

1 c. lemon juice

1 pt. pineapple juice

8 ozs. frozen strawberries

Party Punch
(makes 30 servings)

1 ___gallon___ orange juice

1/2 _____ lemon/lime soda

1 _____ lemon juice

1 _____ pineapple juice

1 _____ frozen strawberries

A   AN INVITATION

Read the invitation. Decide if the sentences are True (T) or False (F).

Please join us as our daughter

Lisa Johnson

graduates from Jameson College
in ceremonies

Saturday, June 1
at 4:00 in the afternoon
Jameson Hall

Party following the ceremony
at our home:
121 Longwood Road
Longwood Lake, Michigan

RSVP by May 19
kjohnson@worldmail.net

_____ 1. Lisa Johnson is graduating from high school.

_____ 2. The party invitation is from Lisa Johnson.

_____ 3. The ceremonies and the party are at the same place.

_____ 4. The party is after the ceremony.

_____ 5. The party is at the Johnsons' house.

_____ 6. The ceremony is in the evening.

_____ 7. You need to answer the invitation by June 1.

_____ 8. You need to answer the invitation by e-mail.

B   NUMERACY: Word Problems with Elapsed Time

Read the invitation and the housing ad. Solve the word problems.

Ann & Peter Lee

invite you to celebrate their

25th Wedding Anniversary

Saturday, June 15 at 6:30 P.M.
Pinelli's Club 324 Lincoln Drive

$500 mo., no utilites

ites

ent.
s.
s

ies

OPEN HOUSE
1 Bedroom Apartment
Sunday June 16
11:00 A.M. – 2:30 P.M.

Hudson Rentals
1440 Wilton Avenue
Apt. 7D

1. The Sterns arrived at the Lees' party at 6:15. How early were they?
   a. 10 minutes early
   b. 15 minutes early
   c. 20 minutes early

2. The Watsons arrived at the Lees' party at 7:10. How late were they?
   a. 20 minutes late
   b. 35 minutes late
   c. 40 minutes late

3. How long is the open house?
   a. 2 hours and 30 minutes
   b. 3 hours
   c. 3 hours and 30 minutes

4. Sam Johnson visited the open house. He stayed from 12:35 to 1:10. How long did he stay?
   a. 25 minutes
   b. 35 minutes
   c. 45 minutes

A READING AN ADVERTISEMENT

Read the refrigerator ad. Decide if the sentences are True (T) or False (F).

Keep Your Cool with Silver Line's New 3000 Refrigerator!

❋ Taller and wider than the 2000 so you can keep more food fresh!

❋ 3 doors make it easier to reach food!

❋ Same power as the 2000, but uses half the energy!

❋ Faster ice maker than the 2000!

❋ Cleaner water than the 2000 with its new five filter cleaning system!

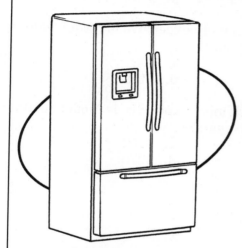

"The Silver Line 3000 is quieter and more efficient than any other large refrigerator."
—*Electric Review*

Price: $2,600

_____ 1. The 2000 is as powerful as the 3000.

_____ 2. The 3000 is more energy-efficient than the 2000.

_____ 3. The 2000 has cleaner water than the 3000.

_____ 4. The 3000 is larger than the 2000.

_____ 5. The 3000 is easier to use than the 2000.

_____ 6. According to the *Electric Review*, the Silver Line 3000 is quieter and more convenient than any other large refrigerator.

_____ 7. According to the ad, bigger is better.

B CONSUMER AWARENESS: Comparing Products Before You Purchase

Finish the paragraph to tell about a product you want to buy—a home appliance, a TV, a cell phone, or something else. Use the comparatives of these adjectives and others in your sentences: *cheap, easy-to-use, expensive, fast, heavy, large, light, powerful, reliable, slow, small*.

I want to buy a _____. I'm comparing two different ones.

I might buy _____ because it's _____

_____.

Or I might buy _____ because it's _____

_____.

C NUMERACY: Using Math to Compare Products

You're looking for a new refrigerator. Look at the information stickers and answer the questions.

```
Refrigerator Model 2000
61 inches high    29½ inches wide
29½ inches deep
▼
Energy cost per year: $78
Price: $847
```

```
Refrigerator Model 3010
64½ inches high    35½ inches wide
32 inches deep
▼
Energy cost per year: $51
Price: $999
```

1. How much higher is Model 3010 than Model 2000?
   a. 2½ inches
   b. 3 inches
   c. 3½ inches
   d. 4½ inches

2. How much wider is Model 3010 than Model 2000?
   a. 5½ inches
   b. 6 inches
   c. 6½ inches
   d. 7 inches

3. How much deeper is Model 3010 than Model 2000?
   a. 2½ inches
   b. 3 inches
   c. 3½ inches
   d. 4 inches

4. How much more expensive is Model 3010 to buy?
   a. $52
   b. $133
   c. $142
   d. $152

5. How much more expensive is Model 2000 to use each year?
   a. $27
   b. $47
   c. $92
   d. $152

6. How much more expensive is Model 2000 to use for 10 years?
   a. $68
   b. $118
   c. $152
   d. $270

D NUMERACY: Word Problems with Comparatives

Solve the word problems.

1. Jim is buying a laptop computer. One model weighs 4½ pounds. The other model weighs 7 pounds. What is their difference in weight?
   a. 1½ pounds
   b. 2½ pounds
   c. 3½ pounds

2. Linda is buying a printer. One printer costs $149.50 and the other costs $185. What is the difference in cost?
   a. $35.50
   b. $40.50
   c. $45.50

3. Paul has a new couch. It's 91 inches wide and 38 inches high. His old couch was 77 inches wide and 34 inches high. How much wider is Paul's new couch?
   a. 4 inches wider
   b. 14 inches wider
   c. 40 inches wider

4. Nancy needs an air conditioner. Model A is $349. Model B is $369. Nancy has a $25 coupon for Model B. Which air conditioner is cheaper?
   a. Air Conditioner A is $5 cheaper.
   b. Air Conditioner A is $20 cheaper.
   c. Air Conditioner B is $5 cheaper.

Look at the clothing labels. Circle T for True and F for False.

L
Men's

100% Polyester

Care instructions
Machine Wash Cold
No Bleach
Tumble Dry Low
Cool Iron

---

1. This clothing item is for men.   T   F

2. You should use only cold water to wash it.   T   F

3. You can use bleach.   T   F

4. You should hang the item to dry it.   T   F

5. You should iron it at a low temperature.   T   F

Ladies
XS
100% Cotton

Care instructions
Machine Wash Warm
Any Bleach
Tumble Dry Normal
Hot Iron

---

6. This clothing item is for women.   T   F

7. You should wash it in a machine.   T   F

8. You should wash it in hot water.   T   F

9. You can use bleach.   T   F

10. You should iron it at a high temperature.   T   F

Girls   **M**
80% Cotton
20% Spandex

Hand wash cold.
Do not bleach.
Dry flat.
Do not dry clean.

---

11. This is children's clothing.   T   F

12. This is medium size.   T   F

13. You should wash it in a machine.   T   F

14. You should put it in a warm dryer.   T   F

15. You should dry clean it.   T   F

Boys

XL

Care instructions
Dry clean only

---

16. This size is extra-small.   T   F

17. You should use only cold water to wash it.   T   F

18. You should wash it by hand.   T   F

19. You should put it in a hot dryer.   T   F

20. You should dry clean it.   T   F

B USING AN ATM

Choose the correct answer.

1. I can't use an ATM if I forget my _____.
   a. PIN
   b. account number
   c. money

2. Which of the following is NOT a transaction?
   a. withdrawal
   b. deposit
   c. ATM

3. I want to see how much money is in my account. Which button do I press?
   a. deposit
   b. balance inquiry
   c. fast cash

4. I want to put money into my account. Which button do I press?
   a. withdrawal
   b. deposit
   c. PIN

5. I want to take money out of my account. Which button do I press?
   a. transfer
   b. deposit
   c. withdrawal

6. I want to move money from one account to another account. Which button do I press?
   a. withdrawal
   b. transfer
   c. balance inquiry

C PARTS OF A CHECK

Look at the check. Answer the questions.

```
Mei Ling                      BELMONT SAVINGS BANK              1103
1217 Water Street
Greenwood, FL 32443                              DATE  8/2/18

PAY TO THE
ORDER OF   Southern Gas Company                      $ 76.04

                            04
           Seventy-six and   /100                         dollars

For   April bill #29530                    Mei Ling
```

1. Who is the check from? _____

2. Who is the check to? _____

3. When did the person write the check? _____

4. How much is the check for? _____

D WRITING CHECKS

Pay $45.10 to Community Telephone Company. Write today's date and sign your name.

```
                    CITYWIDE SAVINGS BANK              101

                                         DATE _____

PAY TO THE
ORDER OF _____   $ _____

_____ dollars

For _____      _____
```

Pay $76.50 to Gray's Department Store. Write today's date and sign your name.

CITYWIDE SAVINGS BANK		102
	DATE _____	
PAY TO THE ORDER OF _____	$ [ ]	
_____ dollars		
For _____ _____		

E NUMERACY: Balancing a Checkbook

Write the check information in the checkbook register and balance the checkbook.

Marie Louis — 151
DATE 4/28/17
PAY TO THE ORDER OF Milton Electric Company $ 53.50
Fifty-three and 50/100 _____ Dollars
For 04-6627-88 ____ Marie Louis
⑆233157221⑆ ⑆2241536?⑈ 151

Marie Louis — 152
DATE 4/28/17
PAY TO THE ORDER OF Star Gas Company $ 45.00
Forty-five and xx/100 _____ Dollars
For 23452-001 ____ Marie Louis
⑆233157221⑆ ⑆2241536?⑈ 152

Marie Louis — 153
DATE 5/1/17
PAY TO THE ORDER OF Benson Realty $ 750.00
Seven hundred fifty and xx/100 _____ Dollars
For May's Rent ____ Marie Louis
⑆233157221⑆ ⑆2241536?⑈ 153

Marie Louis — 154
DATE 5/6/17
PAY TO THE ORDER OF CCS Cable Company $ 110.00
One hundred ten and xx/100 _____ Dollars
For 64-452-02 ____ Marie Louis
⑆233157221⑆ ⑆2241536?⑈ 154

Medical Associates
Payroll Department **MID-CITY BANK** 6258
PAY TO THE ORDER OF: DATE   AMOUNT
Marie Louis   05/07/2017 $1,245.00
123 First Street
Los Angeles, CA 12345
C.W. Wilson
AUTHORIZED SIGNATURE
⑆746599331⑆888234 22⑈6258⑈

Marie Louis — 155
DATE 5/9/17
PAY TO THE ORDER OF United Phone Services $ 84.50
Eighty-four and 50/100 _____ Dollars
For 205-775-3471 ____ Marie Louis
⑆233157221⑆ ⑆2241536?⑈ 155

Number	Date	Transaction	Debit	Credit	Balance
150	4/21	Transworld Credit Card	850.50		753.50
	4/23	Paycheck		1,245.00	1,998.50
151	4/28	Milton Electric Company			
152	4/28		45.00		
153	5/1				
154	5/6				
	5/7	Paycheck		1,245.00	
155	5/9				

A BUSINESS SCHEDULES

Look at the schedules. Complete the sentences.

Barber Shop

Mon	CLOSED	
Tues	9:00	– 6:00
Wed	9:00	– 6:00
Thurs	9:00	– 7:00
Fri	9:00	– 7:00
Sat	8:00	– 6:00
Sun	CLOSED	

MUSEUM

Monday	CLOSED	
Tuesday	CLOSED	
Wednesday	10:00	– 5:00
Thursday	10:00	– 7:00
Friday	10:00	– 5:00
Saturday	10:00	– 6:00
Sunday	12:00	– 5:00

Shopping Mall

M	9:30	– 9:00
T	9:30	– 9:00
W	9:30	– 9:00
Th	9:30	– 9:00
F	9:30	– 10:00
S	9:00	– 10:00
S	12:00	– 6:00

1. On Wednesday the museum opens at _____.

2. On Sunday the mall opens at _____.

3. The barber shop is closed on _____ and _____.

4. The museum is open for _____ hours on Thursday.

5. The museum is closed on _____ and _____.

6. The _____ opens on Saturday at 8:00.

7. The _____ closes on Sunday at 5:00.

8. The _____ closes on Friday at 10:00.

B A TRAIN SCHEDULE

Look at the schedule. Decide if the sentences are True (T) or False (F).

	AM	PM	PM	PM	PM	PM	PM	PM
Kingston	11:15	1:15	3:15	4:15	5:01	5:45	6:15	7:03
Lancaster	11:23	1:23	3:23	4:23	5:09	5:53	6:23	7:11
Billings	11:31	1:31	3:31	4:31	5:17	6:01	6:31	7:19
Winchester	11:42	1:42	3:42	4:42	5:28	6:12	6:42	7:30
Medford	11:48	1:48	3:48	4:48	5:34	6:18	6:48	7:36
Central Station	11:59	1:59	3:59	4:59	5:45	6:29	6:59	7:47

____ 1. It takes one hour to travel from Kingston to Central Station.

____ 2. The morning train gets into Central Station at 7:47 AM.

____ 3. You are on the 1:15 train. You'll get to Central Station at 1:59.

____ 4. You need to meet someone at Central Station at 2:30. You should take the 1:23 train from Lancaster.

____ 5. It's 6:10. The next train leaves Billings in 11 minutes.

____ 6. It's 3:30. The next train leaves Medford at 4:48.

____ 7. It's 12:00. The next train leaves Kingston in one hour and 15 minutes.

____ 8. You need to meet someone in Medford at 7:00. You should take the 6:15 train from Kingston.

____ 9. It's 6:10. The next train leaves Winchester in 12 minutes.

____ 10. It's a quarter to one in Billings. The next train is in 41 minutes.

C NUMERACY: Weights & Measurements for Using Postal Services

Look at the measurement chart. Answer the questions.

ITEM	SHAPE	LENGTH	HEIGHT
Letter		5 inch minimum 11-½ inch maximum	3-½ inch minimum 6-½ inch maximum
Large Envelope		11-½ inch minimum no maximum	6-½ inch minimum no maximum

1. Victor is mailing an item that is 13 inches long and 7 inches high. He's mailing _____.
   a. a letter   b. a large envelope

2. Max is mailing an item that is 11½ inches long and 4 inches high. He's mailing _____.
   a. a letter   b. a large envelope

Look at the weight and rate chart. Write the correct cost.

First-Class Mail ™ Letters & Cards	
Weight	**Rate**
1 oz	$0.41
2 oz	$0.58
3 oz	$0.75
3.5 oz	$0.92

First-Class Mail ™ Large Envelopes			
Weight	**Rate**	**Weight**	**Rate**
1 oz	$0.80	5 oz	$1.48
2 oz	$0.97	6 oz	$1.65
3 oz	$1.14	7 oz	$1.82
4 oz	$1.31	8 oz	$1.99

First-Class Mail ™ Parcels			
Weight	**Rate**	**Weight**	**Rate**
1 oz	$1.13	5 oz	$1.81
2 oz	$1.30	6 oz	$1.98
3 oz	$1.47	7 oz	$2.15
4 oz	$1.64	8 oz	$2.32

3. How much does it cost to mail a 3 ounce letter? _____

4. How much does it cost to mail a 3 ounce large envelope? _____

5. How much does it cost to mail an 8 ounce parcel? _____

6. How much does it cost to mail an 8 ounce large envelope? _____

Look at the chart. Read the questions and choose the correct service.

SERVICE	Express Mail ™	First-Class Mail ™	Priority Mail ™
SHAPE & WEIGHT	 70 lbs or less	 3.5 oz or less 13 oz or less	 13 oz – 70 lbs
SPEED	1–2 days	1–3 days	2–3 days

	Express	First-Class	Priority
7. The package weighs 10 pounds. It must arrive in 1 day.	☐	☐	☐
8. The letter weighs 9 ounces. It can arrive in 2–3 days.	☐	☐	☐
9. The letter weighs 10 ounces. It must arrive in 1 day.	☐	☐	☐
10. The package weighs 14 ounces. It can arrive in 2–3 days.	☐	☐	☐

A HELP WANTED AD ABBREVIATIONS

Write the full words next to the abbreviations.

STUDENT BOOK
PAGES **80a–80f**

evenings	full-time	month	required
excellent	hour	part-time	week
experience	Monday to Friday	preferred	years

1. hr. _____

2. wk. _____

3. mo. _____

4. yrs. _____

5. M–F _____

6. eves. _____

7. req. _____

8. pref. _____

9. exp. _____

10. excel._____

11. FT _____

12. PT _____

B READING HELP WANTED ADS

Read the help wanted ads. Choose the correct answer.

FT Salespeople

2 yrs. exp. req. $1800–$2800/mo. Excel.
benefits. Call Ms. Lima at (812) 595-2115.

PT Dishwasher Needed

Eves. M–F. $9/hr. Exp. pref. Apply in person.
China Palace 229 Bow Street.

---

1. The salespeople have to ____.
   a. send a resume
   b. apply in person
   c. have experience
   d. work part-time

2. The salesperson ad has ____.
   a. the name of the business
   b. the name of the person to call
   c. the work hours
   d. the work days

3. The dishwasher has to ____.
   a. send a resume
   b. have experience
   c. work full-time
   d. apply in person

4. The ad for the dishwasher doesn't have ____.
   a. the number of work hours
   b. the name of the business
   c. the pay
   d. the work days

C A JOB APPLICATION FORM

Fill out this part of an application form with your information.

Application for Employment

Name _____ Position Desired _____

Skills _____

EMPLOYMENT (Current Employment First)

Date (Month/Year)   Employer (NAME & ADDRESS)   Position   Salary

From:
   To: _____

From:
   To: _____

Today's Date _____   Signature _____

D NUMERACY: A Paycheck and a Pay Stub

Look at the paycheck and pay stub. Answer the questions.

Kelsey Company			Jill Higgins Employee No. 5362	Pay Period Ending 10/21/17
Earnings	**Rate**	**Hours**	**This Period**	**Year to Date**
Regular	10.00	40	400.00	16,200.00
Overtime	15.00	5	75.00	1,230.00
Gross Pay			475.00	17,430.00
Taxes & Deductions			**This Period**	**Year to Date**
Federal Tax			45.00	1,845.00
State Tax			20.00	820.00
FICA/Medicare			35.00	1,435.00
Health Plan			40.00	1,600.00
Total			140.00	5,700.00
Net Pay			335.00	11,730.00

Kelsey Company   12398

DATE ___10/21/17___

PAY TO THE
ORDER OF ___JILL HIGGINS___ $ | 335.00 |

Three hundred thirty-five and no/100 _____ Dollars

For _____   *Manuel Espinola*

:746355261 :36455670" 12398

1. How many total hours did Jill work in this pay period? _____

2. How much did the company deduct this period for federal and state taxes? _____

3. How much did Jill pay for federal and state taxes year-to-date? _____

4. How much did the company deduct for FICA (Social Security)/Medicare and Jill's health plan in this pay period? _____

5. How much did Jill pay for FICA (Social Security)/Medicare and her health plan year-to-date? _____

6. Next pay period Jill will work only 35 hours at her regular rate. How much will her gross pay be? _____

7. If Jill works 40 hours at her regular pay rate and 10 hours at her overtime rate, how much money will she make in a week? _____

8. Jill makes $10 an hour in regular pay. Jill earned $16,200 in regular pay year-to-date. How many hours did she work at her regular pay rate year-to-date? _____

9. Next year Jill will get a raise of $.50 an hour. How much will she make in regular pay each week when she works 40 hours a week? _____

E READING AN ACCIDENT REPORT

Read the accident report. Decide if the sentences are True (T) or False (F).

EMPLOYEE ACCIDENT REPORT

Name of injured employee: _Hassan Ali_   SS#: _222-40-6718_ Sex: ✔ M ___ F

Job Title: _Electrician_   Department: _Maintenance_   Date of Report: _04/02/18_

Where did accident occur? _Cafeteria kitchen_   Date of Accident: _3/28/18_

Time of Accident: _6:00_ (A.M.)/P.M. Names of Witnesses: _Paula Spellman_

Nature of injury and part(s) of body injured: _I got a shock in my hand._

How did the employee get injured? _I was installing a dishwasher. I touched a "live" wire._

What safety equipment, if any, did employee use? _boots_

What factors contributed to the accident? _There wasn't enough light. I couldn't see the_
wires very well.

Did employee lose time from work? _Yes_   How much time? _One day_

Immediate Supervisor signature: _Sammy Tate_   Date signed: _04/02/18_

_____ 1. Hassan is a technician.

_____ 2. The accident was in the evening.

_____ 3. Hassan touched a wrong wire and got a shock.

_____ 4. Nobody saw the accident.

_____ 5. Hassan missed one day of work because of the accident.

F FILLING OUT AN ACCIDENT REPORT

Imagine an accident at work. Complete the accident report form.

EMPLOYEE ACCIDENT REPORT

Name of injured employee: _____ SS#: _____ Sex: ____ M ____ F

Home address of employee: _____ Date of Birth: _____

Job Title: _____ Department: _____ Date of Report: _____

Where did accident occur? _____ Date of Accident: _____

Time of Accident: _____ A.M./P.M. Name(s) of Witness(es): _____

Nature of injury and part(s) of body injured: _____

How did the employee get injured? _____

What safety equipment, if any, did employee use? _____

What factors contributed to the accident? _____

Did employee lose time from work? _____ How much time? _____

Immediate Supervisor signature: _____ Date signed: _____

A EMERGENCIES AT HOME

Complete the paragraph with the correct words.

STUDENT BOOK
PAGES **92a–92d**

dial 911	fire extinguisher	smoke detectors
emergency numbers	first-aid kit	utilities

My family is prepared for an emergency at home. There's a list of _____ ¹ next

to the kitchen phone. If anyone gets hurt, there's a _____ ² in the bathroom. If

there's a fire in the kitchen, we have a _____ ³ there. Also, I make sure all our

_____ ⁴ work. I change their batteries twice a year. My husband and I know how

to turn off the _____ ⁵ in the basement. And everyone in my home knows how to

_____ ⁶ if we need an ambulance, police car, or fire truck.

B FIRST-AID

Match the medical emergency with the correct first-aid instruction.

_____ **1.** animal bite   **a.** Put the wound in cool water for 5 minutes.

_____ **2.** bee sting   **b.** Don't touch the person.

_____ **3.** bleeding   **c.** Put ice on the wound.

_____ **4.** burn   **d.** Perform the Heimlich Maneuver.

_____ **5.** choking   **e.** Wash the wound for 5 minutes.

_____ **6.** electric shock   **f.** Apply pressure on the wound for 10 minutes.

C A FIRST-AID KIT

Look at the first-aid kit. Write the correct letter next to the name of each item.

_____ **1.** adhesive tape

_____ **2.** antibiotic ointment

_____ **3.** antiseptic wipe

_____ **4.** bandages

_____ **5.** elastic bandage

_____ **6.** hydrogen peroxide

_____ **7.** pain reliever

_____ **8.** scissors

_____ **9.** tweezers

_____ **10.** sterile dressing pad

D NUMERACY: Reading Statistical Information in Tables

Look at the table about home fires. Decide if the sentences are True (T) or False (F).

Most Common Causes of Home Fires			
Cooking	32%	Another house on fire	4%
Heating System	16%	House electrical or lighting system	3%
Someone starting the fire on purpose	5%	Clothing washer or dryer	2%
Burning candles	4%	Someone playing with fire	2%
Smoking cigarettes	4%	Burning trash in a container	2%

_____ 1. 3% of all home fires begin with burning candles.

_____ 2. Cooking is the most common cause of a home fire.

_____ 3. People start 6 out of 100 home fires on purpose.

_____ 4. 16 out of 100 fires start because of the heating system.

_____ 5. Clothing washers and dryers have the same chance of starting a fire as burning trash.

_____ 6. An electrical or lighting system problem is a more common cause of home fires than smoking cigarettes.

Look at the table about hurricanes. Answer the questions.

State	Number of Hurricanes in 103 Years	Storms Per Year	State	Number of Hurricanes in 103 Years	Storms Per Year
Alabama	11	0.11	Mississippi	9	0.09
Connecticut	8	0.08	North Carolina	29	0.28
Florida	60	0.57	New York	9	0.09
Georgia	5	0.05	Rhode Island	5	0.05
Louisiana	27	0.26	South Carolina	15	0.14
Massachusetts	6	0.06	Texas	37	0.36
Maine	5	0.05	Virginia	4	0.04

7. Which state had 27 storms in 103 years? _____

8. Which states had five hurricanes each in 103 years?

_____

9. Which state had the fewest storms per year? _____

10. Which state had the most storms per year? _____

11. How many more hurricanes did Florida have than Texas in 103 years? _____

12. How many more hurricanes did North Carolina have than South Carolina in 103 years? _____

A INQUIRING ABOUT AN APARTMENT FOR RENT

Complete each question with the correct word.

1. Do you have any one-bedroom apartments _____?

2. How much is the _____ each month?

3. Does that include electricity and other _____?

4. Is there a security _____?

5. Are pets _____?

6. Is _____ for my car included in the rent?

7. Is there a bus stop or other public _____ nearby?

allowed
available
deposit
parking
rent
transportation
utilities

B HOUSING REPAIRS

Write the words on the correct line. You can use some words twice.

1. Things that get clogged: _____

2. Things that leak: _____

3. Things that don't turn on: _____

bathtub
dishwasher
light
sink
stove
toilet

C APARTMENT ADS

Look at the apartment ads. Write the letter of the correct apartment next to each sentence.

A

ESSEX Lg. apt. avail. now.
3 BR, 1.5 BA, liv.rm., mod.
eat-in-kit., new refrig., d/w,
washer & dryer. $1600 plus
util. No pets.
Call supt. 312–555–1629

B

MIDDLETON Sunny 1-BR apt.
1 BA, balc., 4th flr. Elev. in
bldg., a/c, laundry rm. in
bsmt. Pkg. No pets. $850.
Util. incl.
Call mgr. 312–555–0295

C

CENTERVILLE Beaut. 2-BR,
1 BA apt. in 2-fam. hse. Lge.
kit., liv rm., din rm., nr. bus
stop. Pets OK. $1200. Util.
incl.
Call owner. 971–555–1352

_____ 1. It has three bedrooms.

_____ 2. Pets are allowed.

_____ 3. Utilities are not included.

_____ 4. It has a laundry room in the basement.

_____ 5. Call the superintendent to find out more.

_____ 6. It has parking.

_____ 7. It's in a two-family house.

_____ 8. Call the manager to find out more.

_____ 9. It has one and a half bathrooms.

_____ 10. It has air conditioning.

_____ 11. It's near public transportation.

_____ 12. There's a dishwasher in the kitchen.

_____ 13. There's an elevator in the building.

_____ 14. It has a new refrigerator.

D NUMERACY: Square Footage in a Housing Floor Plan

Look at the floor plan and answer the questions.

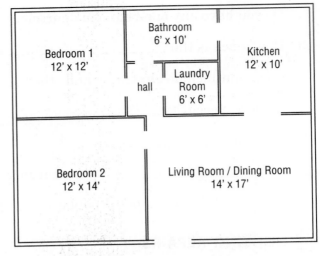

1. What is the biggest room in the apartment?
   a. Bedroom 1
   b. the kitchen
   c. the living room/dining room

2. What is the smallest room in the apartment?
   a. the laundry room
   b. the bathroom
   c. the kitchen

3. How do you find the square footage of Bedroom 1?
   a. 12 feet + 12 feet = 24 square feet
   b. 12 feet × 12 feet = 144 square feet
   c. 14 feet × 14 feet = 196 square feet

4. What is the square footage of the kitchen?
   a. 22 square feet
   b. 60 square feet
   c. 120 square feet

5. What is the square footage of the laundry room?
   a. 12 square feet
   b. 24 square feet
   c. 36 square feet

6. What is the square footage of the bathroom?
   a. 16 square feet
   b. 60 square feet
   c. 600 square feet

E APARTMENT BUILDING RULES AND REGULATIONS

Look at the *Building Rules and Regulations* on student book page 102c. Decide if each statement follows the rules and regulations. Write Y (Yes) or N (No).

_____ 1. Pay your rent with cash.

_____ 2. Have a dance party until 1:00 A.M. in the morning.

_____ 3. Keep hallways and stairs clear.

_____ 4. Lock the door of your apartment whenever you leave.

_____ 5. Give guests the key to your apartment.

_____ 6. Tell the apartment manager if your apartment will be empty for a week.

_____ 7. Disconnect your bathroom fan and smoke detectors.

_____ 8. Tell the apartment manager when there is a problem with your smoke detector.

_____ 9. Take your laundry out of the machine promptly.

_____ 10. The laundry room is for you and your friends to use.

_____ 11. Store bicycles and other personal belongings on your balcony.

_____ 12. Keep your pet in your apartment.

_____ 13. Park on the driveway.

_____ 14. Talk to the landlord before you install a satellite dish.

_____ 15. Use large nails to hang pictures on the apartment walls.

A PARTS OF THE FACE

Write the correct word on each line.

| cheek | eye | forehead | lip | teeth |
| chin | eyebrow | jaw | nose | tongue |

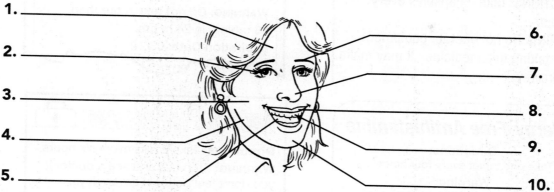

1. _____

2. _____

3. _____

4. _____

5. _____

6. _____

7. _____

8. _____

9. _____

10. _____

B PARTS OF THE BODY

Write the correct word on each line.

ankle	elbow	hand	knee	throat
arm	finger	head	neck	toes
chest	foot	hip	shoulder	wrist

1. _____

2. _____

3. _____

4. _____

5. _____

6. _____

7. _____

8. _____

9. _____

10. _____

11. _____

12. _____

13. _____

14. _____

15. _____

READING MEDICINE LABELS

Look at the medicine labels. Answer the questions.

Breathe Clear Decongestant

DIRECTIONS: Take 2 capsules every six hours.
WARNING: Do not operate equipment while taking this medicine. It may make you drowsy.

TYLER ANTACID TABLETS

Dosage: two to four tablets as needed
WARNING: Do not take more than 16 tablets in 24 hours.
Expiration Date: 03/19

Allergy-Free Antihistamine
Directions:
Take one tablet every four hours.
Warning:
Do not take more than six tablets in 24 hours.
Use before 08/20

ADDISON PAIN MEDICINE

Directions: Take 2 pills every six hours.
WARNING: Stop use and see a doctor if you don't feel better in seven days.
Side effects: May upset stomach.

1. What's the dosage of the decongestant? _____

2. What are the side effects of the pain medicine? _____

3. What's the expiration date of the antihistamine? _____

4. What's the dosage of the antihistamine? _____

5. How many antacid tablets can you take in 24 hours? _____

6. What is the last date you can use the antacid tablets? _____

7. How much antihistamine can you take in 24 hours? _____

8. What's the dosage of the pain medicine? _____

9. What are the side effects of the decongestant? _____

D **NUTRITION: Categorizing Nutrients and Foods**

Write the following foods and nutrients in the correct categories.

| beans | cereal | fish | low-fat milk | mayonnaise | rice |
| calcium | desserts | fried foods | low-fat yogurt | potassium | soda |

Protein: _____   **Bad Fats:** _____

Sugar: _____   **Grains:** _____

Dairy: _____   **Minerals:** _____

 158 Activity Workbook

Alex is making a party fruit drink. He only has a teaspoon and a 1-pint measure. Read the chart and answer the questions.

3 teaspoons = 1 tablespoon	1 cup = 1/2 pint
4 tablespoons = 1/4 cup	2 cups = 1 pint
8 tablespoons = 1/2 cup	2 pints = 1 quart
12 tablespoons = 3/4 cup	4 quarts = 1 gallon

1. The recipe requires 2 tablespoons of lemon juice. How many teaspoons is that?
   a. 2 teaspoons
   b. 4 teaspoons
   c. 6 teaspoons

2. The recipe requires 1/4 cup of sugar. How many teaspoons is that?
   a. 6 teaspoons
   b. 12 teaspoons
   c. 24 teaspoons

3. The recipe requires a cup of pineapple juice. How many pints is that?
   a. 1/2 pint
   b. 1 pint
   c. 1 1/2 pints

4. The recipe requires 2 quarts of orange juice. How many pints is that?
   a. 2 pints
   b. 3 pints
   c. 4 pints

F NUMERACY: Adjusting a Recipe

Read the recipe and answer the questions.

 Pancake Recipe

For 12 pancakes
2 eggs
2 cups milk
1 teaspoon salt
3 cups flour
3 teaspoons baking powder
2 tablespoons oil

Mix the flour, baking powder, and salt together.
Mix the egg, milk, and oil together. Mix the wet and dry ingredients together.
For each pancake, pour a 1/4 cup of mixture in a hot pan.

1. What is the recipe for 6 pancakes? (Do half the recipe above.)
   _____ egg
   _____ cup milk
   _____ teaspoon salt
   _____ cups flour
   _____ teaspoons baking powder
   _____ tablespoon oil

2. What is the recipe for 24 pancakes? (Double the recipe above.)
   _____ eggs
   _____ pints milk
   _____ teaspoons salt
   _____ cups flour
   _____ tablespoons baking powder
   _____ cup oil

A A TELEPHONE DIRECTORY

Look at the telephone listings. Choose the correct answer.

			RIV–ROF	528
RIVER	**Tom**	200 Plain View Cla	....	517–593–9827
	Victor	2925 Washington Av Gre	....	231–257–6821
RIVERA	**A & J**	780 Central Cli	....	517–897–0081
	Dennis	30 Broad Arc	....	231–257–1171
	Teresa	175 Federal Can	....	734–545–9338
RIVES	**D**	32 Grant Cla	....	517–593–2451
RIVKIN	**Natalie**	32 Pine Arc	....	231–257–2451
RIZZO	**Anthony**	1480 Main She	....	517–593–2451
	C & E	1770 Oak Roc	....	734–545–0095

1. Alice and Jake Rivera live in _____ .
   a. Clayton   c. Clinton
   b. Canton   d. Greenville

2. The area code for Rockwood is _____ .
   a. 743   c. 231
   b. 517   d. 734

3. The phone number for _____ is on a different page.
   a. Liz Roach   c. Joan Rodriquez
   b. Bill Rogers   d. William Robson

4. Natalie Rivkin lives in _____ .
   a. Arcadia   c. Redford
   b. Canton   d. Clayton

5. Charles and Ellen Rizzo live on _____ .
   a. Main Street   c. Oak Street
   b. Federal Street   d. Plain View Avenue

6. Victor River's phone number is _____ .
   a. 231-275-6821   c. 517-593-9827
   b. 517-897-0081   d. 231-257-6821

B THE YELLOW PAGES

Look at the yellow page listings. Decide if the sentences on the next page are True (T) or False (F).

BAGELS

Bagel Land
 21 Davis Avenue, Fairfield .... (352) 889–1327

Bob's Bagels – see our ad this page
 24 High Street, Melrose .... (352) 298–9911

BAGS

The Packaging Store
 52 Medford Way, Webster .... (352) 298–4545

BAKERIES

Cake Walk
 167 Common Avenue, Fairfield .... (352) 298–6162

Dolly's Donuts – see our ad this page
 52 Lakeview Road, Webster .... (352) 298–5067

Whole Desserts – see our ad this page
 21 Lewiston Ave, Melrose .... (352) 889–6590

Bob's Bagels

The freshest in town!
Try our new raisin nut bagel.

Open 5:00 AM – 3:00 PM every day
We also serve Coffee, Soup, & Sandwiches
24 High Street, Melrose (352) 298–9911

DOLLY'S DONUTS

Fried fresh for you!

Open 24 hours!
"The best donuts in town!"
52 Lakeview Road, Webster (352) 298–5067

WHOLE DESSERTS
WHOLE WHEAT BREAD, FRUIT CAKE
WHOLE GRAIN COOKIES, LOW-FAT APPLE CAKE
6:00 AM – 4:00 PM MONDAY – SATURDAY
21 LEWISTON AVE MELROSE (352) 889–6590

_____ 1. Dolly's Donuts is open at 3:00 in the morning.

_____ 2. Whole Desserts is open every day.

_____ 3. Bob's Bagels serves lunch.

_____ 4. The address of the bagel store in Melrose is 21 Davis Avenue.

_____ 5. Dolly's Donuts is in Webster.

_____ 6. The phone number for The Packaging Store is 325-298-4545.

_____ 7. Whole Desserts sells donuts.

_____ 8. The phone number for the bakery in Fairfield is 352-298-6590.

C A TELEPHONE BILL

Look at the telephone bill. Choose the correct answer.

Peter Wong
123 Jefferson Road
Medfield, MA 02052

Account Number: 2354768829
Phone Number: 508-555-2834
Billing Period: 10/04/18–11/03/18
Billing Date: 11/04/18

ACCOUNT SUMMARY

Amount of Last Bill	$39.50	Current Charges	
Payment Thank You	39.50	Local Monthly Charges	$ 33.25
Balance	$ 0.00	Long Distance Service Charges	16.06
		Amount due on 11/22/18	$ 49.31

LOCAL TELEPHONE SERVICE

Local Unlimited Calling	$ 22.00	Federal Tax	$ 0.62
Line Charge	6.50	State and Local Surcharge	0.32
Federal Tax	2.25	Single Bill Fee	2.35
State and Local Taxes	2.50	Long Distance Calls	12.77
Total Local Charges	$ 33.25	Total Long Distance Charges	$ 16.06

LONG DISTANCE SERVICE

DATE	TIME	PLACE AND NUMBER CALLED		TYPE	RATE	MINUTES	AMOUNT
10/04/18	7:05 P.M.	LA, CA	(213) 555-1769	Direct	Night	12	1.20
10/11/18	11:12 A.M.	NYC, NY	(212) 555-9573	Direct	Day	2	0.50
10/12/18	5:48 P.M.	Dallas, TX	(972) 222-8609	Direct	Day	18	4.50
10/28/18	12:28 P.M.	Phil, PA	(445) 222-9678	Direct	Day	31	2.79
11/02/18	9:51 P.M.	Miami, FL	(305) 444-2781	Direct	Night	42	3.78

1. What is Peter Wong's account number?
   a. 2354768829
   b. 508-555-2834
   c. 02052

2. How long is the billing period?
   a. a week
   b. two weeks
   c. a month

3. When is the bill due?
   a. 10/04/18
   b. 11/04/18
   c. 11/22/18

4. How much was Peter's last phone bill?
   a. $22.00
   b. $39.50
   c. $6.50

5. How much is this phone bill?
   a. $16.06
   b. $33.25
   c. $49.31

6. How much are the long distance charges?
   a. $16.06
   b. $33.25
   c. $49.31

7. How many long distance phone calls did Peter make between 10/04 and 11/03?
   a. 4
   b. 5
   c. 6

D NUMERACY: Fahrenheit & Celsius Temperatures

Look at the thermometer and match the temperatures.

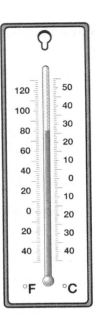

____	**1.** 32° F	**a.**	15° C
____	**2.** 90° F	**b.**	32° C
____	**3.** 50° F	**c.**	0° C
____	**4.** 14° F	**d.**	27° C
____	**5.** 80° F	**e.**	−10° C
____	**6.** 0° F	**f.**	10° C
____	**7.** 60° F	**g.**	−16° C

F NUMERACY: Word Problems with Elapsed Time

Choose the correct answer.

1. It's 8:15 A.M. Josh will be driving until 1:00 P.M. How much longer will he be driving?
   a. 3 hours and 45 minutes
   b. 4 hours and 15 minutes
   c. 4 hours and 45 minutes

2. It's 11 P.M. Pam will be working until 6:30 A.M. How much longer will she be working?
   a. 7 1/2 hours
   b. 8 hours
   c. 8 1/2 hours

3. It's 10:45 A.M. Debbie will be exercising until 11:25. How much longer will she be exercising?
   a. 30 minutes
   b. 40 minutes
   c. 45 minutes

4. It's 11:45 A.M. Kerry will be working for 3 1/2 more hours. When will she stop working?
   a. 2:30 P.M.
   b. 3:00 P.M.
   c. 3:15 P.M.

5. It's 5:45 P.M. Andy's cake needs to bake for 55 more minutes. When will he be taking the cake out of the oven?
   a. 6:40 P.M.
   b. 6:45 P.M.
   c. 6:50 P.M.

6. It's 9:10 A.M. Students will be taking a test for the next 3 hours and 45 minutes. What time will the test end?
   a. 12:55 P.M.
   b. 12:55 P.M.
   c. 1:35 P.M.

Read the Rental Agreement. Decide if the sentences are True (T) or False (F).

Rental Agreement

THIS AGREEMENT IS BETWEEN:

_____ Carlos Mesa _____ as LANDLORD and _____ Alison Worth _____ as TENANT. The LANDLORD leases to the TENANT apartment number : __2A__ at ___115 Broadway___ Fairmont, Maine 04263 for the term of ____twelve months____ beginning __September 1, 2018__ and ending on ___August 31, 2019___ .

TERMS AND CONDITIONS OF THIS AGREEMENT:

1. **RENT:** The total rent for the apartment is __$9,000.00__ . The monthly rent is __$750.00__ due on or before the ____first____ day of each month.

2. **UTILITIES AND SERVICES:** The TENANT will pay the following utility and service charges:
   ___Electricity, Telephone, and Internet___
   The LANDLORD will pay the following utility and service charges:
   ___Gas and Water___

3. **APPLIANCES:** The apartment is rented with the following appliances:
   ___Refrigerator and Dishwasher___
   The LANDLORD will repair appliances that the LANDLORD owns. The TENANT is responsible for repairing any other appliances.

4. **SECURITY DEPOSIT:** The TENANT will deposit with the LANDLORD a security deposit of __$1,500.00__ . If the apartment is in good condition when the TENANT moves out, and all rent is paid, the LANDLORD will return the full amount of the security deposit within 30 days.

5. **ENTRY TO APARTMENT:** The LANDLORD has the right to enter the apartment if the LANDLORD gives 24-hour notice.

6. **CONDITION OF APARTMENT:** The TENANT agrees to take good care of the apartment. When the agreement ends, the TENANT will return the apartment in good clean condition.

_____ 1. The security deposit is two months' rent.

_____ 2. The tenant pays for gas and electricity.

_____ 3. The landlord will repair the dishwasher.

_____ 4. The landlord can come into the apartment if he calls first.

_____ 5. The rent is $9,000 a month.

_____ 6. When the agreement ends, the tenant must leave the apartment clean and in good condition.

B TENANTS' RIGHTS AND RESPONSIBILITIES

Read *Know Your Rights* on student book page 136c. Who is responsible? Read the sentences and write L for the landlord and T for the tenant.

_____ 1. Provide an apartment with heating, plumbing, and electricity in working condition.

_____ 2. Keep the building and the land around it clean.

_____ 3. Keep the apartment clean.

_____ 4. Make sure all locks on windows and doors work.

_____ 5. Pay the rent.

_____ 6. Fix problems that make the apartment unhealthy and unsafe.

C NUMERACY: Word Problems about Rent with Multiple Operations

Read the apartment ads. Answer the questions.

Large 2 BEDROOM APARTMENT
Sunny kitchen and dining room. New appliances. $1,200/month. 12-month lease. 1 month security deposit required. Available NOW. 1438 Central Ave. 426-763-9900.

1 BEDROOM APARTMENT NEAR PARK
Large living room. Washer and dryer in basement. $900 monthly rent. Security deposit: 2 months rent. Two-year lease. Avail. 7/1/17.

1. How much will someone pay for a year of rent in the two-bedroom apartment?
   a. $12,000
   b. $14,400
   c. $24,000

2. Three friends are looking at the two-bedroom apartment. If they rent it, they will share the cost equally. How much will each person pay per month?
   a. $300
   b. $400
   c. $4,800

3. The Carters rented the apartment. They paid a plumber $175 to repair the kitchen sink, and they deducted this amount from last month's rent. How much rent did they pay last month?
   a. $925
   b. $975
   c. $1,025

4. The Carters will stay in this apartment next year, but they will have to pay an additional 10% for the rent. How much will the monthly rent be next year?
   a. $1,320
   b. $1,380
   c. $1,410

5. How much will someone pay for a year of rent in the one-bedroom apartment?
   a. $9,900
   b. $10,600
   c. $10,800

6. How much is the security deposit?
   a. $1,350
   b. $1,800
   c. $1,900

7. Ana rented the apartment from the first day it was available. When does her lease end?
   a. 06/30/18
   b. 06/30/19
   c. 06/30/20

8. Ana paid a locksmith $250 to fix the apartment door lock. She deducted this amount from last month's rent. How much rent did she pay last month?
   a. $650
   b. $700
   c. $750

APPENDIX

Listening Scripts

Listen and choose the correct response.

1. What do your friends like to do on the weekend?
2. What does your sister like to do on the weekend?
3. What does your brother like to do on the weekend?
4. What do you and your friends like to do on the weekend?
5. What does your son like to do on the weekend?
6. What do you like to do on the weekend?
7. What does your next-door neighbor like to do on the weekend?
8. What does your cousin Sue like to do on the weekend?

Page 10 Exercise N

Listen and write the ordinal number you hear.

Many people live and work in this large apartment building in New York City.

1. There's a barber shop on the second floor.
2. The Wong family lives on the twelfth floor.
3. The Acme Internet Company is on the thirtieth floor.
4. Bob Richards lives on the thirteenth floor.
5. There's a bank on the third floor.
6. There's a dentist's office on the ninth floor.
7. There's a flower shop on the first floor.
8. The Martinez family lives on the nineteenth floor.
9. Louise Lane works on the seventeenth floor.
10. There's a computer store on the fourth floor.
11. There's an expensive French restaurant on the forty-eighth floor.
12. My apartment is on the fifth floor.
13. The Park family lives on the thirty-fourth floor.
14. Dr. Jacobson has an office on the twenty-sixth floor.
15. The Walker family lives on the sixty-second floor.
16. There's a health club on the eighteenth floor.

Page 13 Exercise C

Listen and choose the correct response.

1. Where's the tea?
2. Where are the oranges?
3. Where's the fish?
4. Where are the cookies?
5. Where's the cake?
6. Where's the rice?
7. Where are the pears?
8. Where's the cheese?

Page 15 Exercise F

Listen and put a check under the correct picture.

1. Let's have some pizza!
2. Where are the eggs?
3. Let's make some fresh orange juice!
4. Let's bake a pie!
5. Where are the potatoes?
6. Let's have a sandwich for lunch!

Page 19 Exercise L

Listen and put a check under the correct picture.

1. A. Would you care for some more?
   B. Yes, please. But not too much.
2. A. Do you like them?
   B. Yes, but my doctor says that too many are bad for my health.
3. A. These are wonderful!
   B. I'm glad you like them. I bought them this morning.
4. A. How much did you eat?
   B. I ate too much!
5. A. I bought it this morning, and it's very good. Would you like a little?
   B. Yes, please.
6. A. I really don't like them.
   B. But they're good for you!
7. A. How do you like them?
   B. They're wonderful.
8. A. Would you care for some more?
   B. Yes, please. But not too much.
9. A. Hmm. This is delicious. Would you care for some more?
   B. Yes, please. But just a little.
10. A. This is delicious!
    B. I'm glad you like it. I made it this morning.

Page 22 Exercise C

Listen to the conversations. Put a check under the foods you hear.

1. A. Do we need anything from the supermarket?
   B. Yes. We need a pound of apples, a bunch of bananas, and a head of lettuce.
2. A. What do we need at the supermarket?
   B. We need a pound of cheese, a box of rice, and a bottle of soda.
3. A. Do we need anything from the supermarket?
   B. Yes. We need a loaf of bread, a pound of onions, and a dozen oranges.
4. A. What do we need at the supermarket?
   B. We need a pound of potatoes, a pint of ice cream, and a jar of mustard.

Page 24 Exercise F

Listen and circle the price you hear.

1. A box of cereal costs a dollar ninety-nine.
2. Two cans cost five dollars.
3. Three jars cost four dollars and seventy-nine cents.
4. It costs twenty-five cents.
5. A bottle costs two forty-seven.
6. Two boxes cost six dollars and sixty cents.
7. Three thirteen?! That's a lot of money!
8. A pound costs a dollar fifty.
9. Two dollars and ten cents?! That's cheap!

Page 27 Exercise M

Listen and choose the correct word to complete the sentence.

1. Add a little . . .
2. Chop up a few . . .
3. Cut up a few . . .
4. Pour in a little . . .
5. Slice a few . . .
6. Mix in a little . . .

Page 29 Exercise E

Listen and circle the correct word.

Ex. I want some lemons.
1. I'd like some ice cream.
2. I need some tomatoes.
3. I'm looking for lettuce.
4. May I have some meatballs?
5. I want some whole wheat bread.

Page 32 Exercise D

Listen and circle the words you hear.

1. I want to have the chocolate ice cream.
2. They won't fax the letter this morning.
3. I want to recommend the fish today.
4. Peter and William won't go home this morning.
5. She won't eat meat.
6. They want to get married soon.
7. He won't buy a car this year.
8. We want to use our computer now.

Page 37 Exercise K

Listen and choose the correct answer.

1. I'm afraid I might get sick!
2. I'm afraid I might fall asleep!
3. I'm afraid I might step on your feet!
4. I'm afraid I might break my leg!
5. I'm afraid I might catch a cold!
6. I'm afraid I might drown.
7. I'm afraid I might get seasick!
8. I'm afraid I might get a sunburn!
9. I'm afraid I might have a terrible time!
10. I'm afraid I might look terrible!

Page 42 Exercise F

Listen and choose the correct words to complete the sentences.

1. A. Yesterday was cool.
   B. I know. But today is . . .
2. A. Ronald is tall.
   B. You're right. But his son Jim is . . .
3. A. This briefcase is very attractive.
   B. Really? I think THAT briefcase is . . .
4. A. Nancy is very nice.
   B. Do you know her sister Sally? She's . . .
5. A. Tom is very fast.
   B. You're right. But his brother John is . . .
6. A. Michael is a very friendly person.
   B. I know. But his wife is . . .
7. A. Your roommate is very interesting.
   B. You're right. But I think your roommate is . . .
8. A. The supermarket on Center Street was very busy today.
   B. Yes, I know. But the supermarket on Main Street was . . .

Page 44 Exercise I

Listen and circle the correct answer.

1. Yesterday was hotter than today.
2. The tomatoes are more expensive than the potatoes.
3. Aunt Betty is younger than cousin Jane.
4. Bob is shorter and heavier than Bill.
5. Barry's chair is more comfortable than Larry's chair.
6. The science test was more difficult than the history test.
7. Irene's office is bigger than Eileen's office.
8. Ronald is more capable than Donald.

Page 56 Exercise F

Listen and circle the words you hear.

1. My new chair is much more comfortable than my old chair.
2. Is that the worst city in the country?
3. I want a more energetic president.
4. Don't you have a cheaper one?
5. What was the most important day in your life?
6. Roger is the sloppiest teenager I know.
7. This is the best perfume we have.
8. Sally isn't as lazy as Richard is.
9. You know, I think your dog is meaner than mine.
10. Howard is the most honest person I know.

Page 59 Exercise G

Listen and circle the correct answer.

Ex. Ronald is younger than Fred.
1. Bob is neater than Bill.
2. The chicken is more expensive than the fish.
3. Moscow is warmer than Miami.
4. Herbert is taller than Steven.
5. Patty is more talented than Pam.

Page 63 Exercise D

Look at the map on page 62. Listen and choose the correct answer.

1. Linda was at the hotel on Ninth Avenue. She walked along Ninth Avenue to Elm Street and turned right. She walked up Elm Street to Eighth Avenue and turned right again. She went to a building on the left, between the flower shop and the post office.

2. Roger was at the shoe store on Eighth Avenue. He walked along Eighth Avenue to Oak Street and turned right. He walked down Oak Street and went to a building on the left, across from the parking garage.

3. Mr. and Mrs. Baker were at the book store on Elm Street. They walked up Elm Street to Eighth Avenue and turned right. They walked along Eighth Avenue to a building next to the pet shop and across from the post office.

4. Wanda was at the department store on Ninth Avenue. She walked along Ninth Avenue to Oak Street and turned left. She walked up Oak Street to a building on the right, next to the toy store and across from the library.

5. Alan was at the motel on Oak Street. He walked down Oak Street to Ninth Avenue and turned right. He walked along Ninth Avenue to a place on the left, next to the supermarket and across from the department store.

6. Alice was at the supermarket on Ninth Avenue. She walked along Ninth Avenue to Oak Street and turned left. She walked up Oak Street to Eighth Avenue and turned right. She went to a building on the left, across from the restaurant.

Page 67 Exercise I

Listen and fill in the correct places.

1. David took the Bay Avenue bus and got off at Second Street. He walked up Second Street to Brighton Boulevard and turned right. He walked along Brighton Boulevard to a building on the right, across from the post office. Where did he go?

2. Barbara took the Day Street bus and got off at Second Street. She walked down Second Street to Bay Avenue and turned right. She walked along Bay Avenue to a building between the flower shop and the church. Where did she go?

3. Mr. and Mrs. Jackson took the Bay Avenue bus and got off at First Street. They walked up First Street to Brighton Boulevard and turned left. They walked along Brighton Boulevard to a building on the right, next to the bus station and across from the barber shop. Where did they go?

4. Susan didn't want to take the bus this morning. She was at the library on Bay Avenue. She walked along Bay Avenue to Third Street and turned left. She walked up Third Street to Day Street and turned left again. She walked along Day Street and went to a building on the left, between First Street and Second Street. Where did she go?

5. Mr. and Mrs. Yamamoto wanted to get some exercise this morning. They took the Day Street bus and got off at First Street. They walked down First Street to Brighton Boulevard and turned left. They walked along Brighton Boulevard to Second Street and turned right. They walked down Second Street to Bay Avenue and turned right again. They went to a place on the right, at the corner of First Street and Bay Avenue, next to the concert hall. Where did they go?

6. George got lost this morning. He took the Bay Avenue bus and got off at First Street. He walked up First Street to Brighton Boulevard and turned right. He walked along Brighton Boulevard to Second Street and turned left. He walked up Second Street to Day Street and turned right. He walked along Day Street to Third Street and turned right again. He walked down Third Street to Brighton Boulevard, and then he was happy. He went to a place at the corner of Third Street and Brighton Boulevard, next to the post office and across from the pet shop. Where did he go?

Page 69 Exercise C

Listen and circle the correct word to complete the sentence.

1. He's a good worker, but he's . . .
2. She's an excellent violinist. She plays the violin . . .
3. I don't think he's an honest card player. To tell the truth, everybody says he's . . .
4. I can't read their homework because they write very . . .

(continued)

5. Maria never makes mistakes. She's very . . .
6. Their son Marvin is very polite. He never speaks . . .
7. When you leave the party, please drive home . . .
8. Their car is very old. I don't think it's . . .
9. People can't hear you very well when you speak . . .
10. We never buy expensive clothes. We live very . . .
11. You rode your motorcycle carelessly yesterday. That's strange. You usually ride it very . . .
12. Everybody in the store likes Jane. She works hard, and when she talks to customers she's very . . .

Page 80 Exercise F

Listen and fill in the correct places.

1. Mrs. Mendoza was at the hotel at the corner of First Avenue and Grove Street. She walked up Grove Street to Second Avenue and turned left. She walked along Second Avenue to a building on the left, between the pet shop and the cafeteria. Where did she go?

2. Edward was at the football stadium on First Avenue. He walked along First Avenue to Elm Street and turned left. He walked up Elm Street to Second Avenue and turned right. He walked along Second Avenue to a building on the right, at the corner of Grove Street and Second Avenue, across from the bank. Where did he go?

3. Mr. and Mrs. Wong were at the post office on Second Avenue. They walked along Second Avenue to Grove Street and turned left. They walked down Grove Street to First Avenue and turned right. They went to a building on the left, across from the museum and the parking garage. Where did they go?

4. Thomas was at the hospital on Second Avenue. He walked along Second Avenue to Elm Street and turned right. He walked down Elm Street to First Avenue and turned left. He walked along First Avenue to a building on the left, at the corner of Grove Street and First Avenue, across from the supermarket. Where did he go?

5. Maria was at the shoe store on First Avenue. She walked along First Avenue to Grove Street and turned left. She walked up Grove Street to Second Avenue and turned left again. She walked along Second Avenue to a building on the right, between the toy store and the barber shop, across from the ice cream shop. Where did she go?

Page 83 Exercise E

Listen and choose the correct answer.

1. A. What was he doing yesterday when the lights went out?
   B. He was shaving.
2. A. What was she doing yesterday when you saw her?
   B. She was skating.
3. A. What were they doing when it started to rain?
   B. They were swimming at the beach.
4. A. What was he doing yesterday when you called?
   B. He was studying math.
5. A. What were you doing when your friends arrived?
   B. We were eating.
6. A. What was she doing when you saw her?
   B. She was talking with her mother.
7. A. What was he doing when you called?
   B. He was taking a shower.
8. A. What were you doing when the guests arrived?
   B. I was sweeping the living room.

Page 84 Exercise G

Listen and put the number under the correct picture.

1. I saw you yesterday at about 3:00. You were walking into the bank.
2. I saw you yesterday at about 1:30. You were jogging through the park.
3. I saw you yesterday at about 2:00. You were getting off the D Train.
4. I saw you yesterday at about 5:00. You were getting on the B Train.
5. I saw you yesterday at about 4:45. You were getting out of a taxi on Fifth Street.
6. I saw you yesterday at about noon. You were getting into a taxi on Sixth Street.
7. I saw you yesterday at about 11:45. You were getting on a bus.
8. I saw you yesterday at about 9:00. You were getting off a bus.

Page 88 Exercise M

Listen and choose the correct answer.

1. A. Why does Sally look so upset?
   B. She lost her new boot.
2. A. What happened to Howard?
   B. He burned himself while he was cooking.
3. A. When did you see them?
   B. While they were walking out of the park.
4. A. You look upset. What happened?
   B. Someone stole our new fan.

5. A. I had a bad day today.
   B. Why? What happened?
   A. I dropped my new CD player.
6. A. What happened to Charlie?
   B. A dog bit him while he was walking.
7. A. What were you doing when the accident happened?
   B. We were driving over a bridge.
8. A. What happened to Helen?
   B. She tripped and fell on the kitchen floor.
9. A. When did they drop their packages?
   B. While they were walking up the stairs.
10. A. What was Jane doing when she hurt herself?
    B. She was cooking on the barbecue.
11. A. You look upset. What's the matter?
    B. I cut myself while I was chopping.
12. A. What happened to Fred?
    B. He fainted at the bus stop.

Page 98 Exercise K

Listen to each story, and then choose the correct answers to the questions you hear.

William's New Apartment

William is having problems with his new apartment. Yesterday he was very frustrated. It was a hot day, and he wasn't able to open his living room windows. And today he's upset because all the lights in his apartment went out. William is very disappointed. Now he won't be able to cook dinner or watch his favorite programs on TV.

1. Why was William frustrated yesterday?
2. Why is he upset today?
3. Why is he disappointed?

Mr. and Mrs. Clark's New Computer

Mr. and Mrs. Clark are having problems with their new computer. Yesterday they were frustrated because they couldn't assemble the computer easily. And today they're upset because the computer crashed. Mr. and Mrs. Clark are very disappointed. Now they won't be able to send any e-mail to their grandchildren.

4. Why were Mr. and Mrs. Clark frustrated yesterday?
5. Why are they upset today?
6. Why are they disappointed?

Page 102 Exercise E

Listen to the story, and then choose the correct answers to the questions you hear.

Poor Janet!

Last year Janet's teacher said she couldn't dance in the school play because she was too clumsy. Janet was very upset. This year Janet practiced every day, and now she dances much better. Unfortunately, last week she fell down while she was dancing and she hurt herself. Janet is very disappointed. She won't be able to dance in the play this year.

1. Why was Janet upset last year?
2. What did Janet do this year?
3. What happened while Janet was dancing last week?
4. Why is Janet disappointed?

Page 109 Exercise J

Listen and choose the correct answer.

1. Mr. Lopez, I'm really worried about your eyes.
2. Mrs. Parker, I'm concerned about your heart.
3. I saw my doctor today, and she's concerned about my stomach.
4. Ms. Smith, I'm worried about your blood pressure.
5. Ricky, I'm concerned about your hearing.
6. I saw my doctor today, and he's concerned about my knees.

Page 115 Exercise E

Listen and choose the correct answer.

1. A. What will Betty be doing this afternoon?
   B. She'll be ironing dresses.
2. A. What will Sally and Tom be doing this morning?
   B. They'll be working downtown.
3. A. What will your husband be doing today?
   B. He'll be knitting on the front porch.
4. A. Will you be busy tonight?
   B. Yes, I will. I'll be watching sports.
5. A. Will you and Frank be busy in a half hour?
   B. Yes, we will. We'll be feeding the baby.
6. A. What will Charles be doing later tonight?
   B. He'll be taking a bath.
7. A. Will you and your husband be home this morning?
   B. Yes, we will. We'll be home all morning. We'll be baking cakes.
8. A. Will your daughter be busy this afternoon?
   B. Yes, she will. She'll be doing her homework.
9. A. What will Teddy and Timmy be doing this Sunday morning?
   B. I'm sure they'll be sleeping all morning.
10. A. Will your daughter be home this afternoon?
    B. No, she won't. She'll be skateboarding in the park.
11. A. Will you and your wife be busy this afternoon?
    B. Yes, we will. I think we'll be walking the dog.
12. A. I'm sad that you're leaving.
    B. I know. But don't worry. I'll be thinking about you all the time.

Page 122 Exercise E

Listen to each conversation, and then choose the correct answers to the questions you hear.

Conversation 1

A. I just found this brown wallet on my desk. Is it yours?

B. No. It isn't mine. But it might be John's. He lost his last Tuesday.

A. Thanks. I'll call him right away.

B. I hope it's his. He was very upset when he lost it.

   1. Where was the wallet?

   2. Is the wallet John's?

   3. When did John lose it?

Conversation 2

A. Hello, John? This is Jane. I just found a brown wallet on my desk at work. Is it yours?

B. No. Unfortunately, it isn't mine. Mine is black. But it might be Mary's. She lost hers, too.

A. Okay. I'll call her right away.

B. I hope it's hers. She was very upset when she lost it.

   4. What color is John's wallet?

   5. What did Mary lose at work?

   6. Is the wallet Mary's?

Page 126 Exercise H

Listen and choose the correct response.

1. How was the prom last Saturday?
2. How was your new tuxedo?
3. Was there any good music?
4. How late did you stay?
5. Why did you leave so early?
6. Do you think next year's prom will be better?

Page 129 Exercise L

Listen and choose the person you should call.

1. A. I'm having trouble with my new car!
   B. You should call . . .

2. A. There's water on my bathroom floor!
   B. You should call . . .

3. A. My keys won't open the door lock!
   B. You should call . . .

4. A. My upstairs neighbor lifts weights at two o'clock in the morning!
   B. You should call . . .

5. A. The lights in my kitchen won't go on!
   B. You should call . . .

6. A. Someone stole my bicycle!
   B. You should call . . .

7. A. I can't turn off my kitchen faucet!
   B. You should call . . .

8. A. My computer crashes every day!
   B. You should call . . .

Exercise D Page 133

Listen and choose the correct answers to complete the sentences.

1. Good morning. I'm Doctor Johnson. Today I'll be giving you . . .
2. First, you'll stand on a scale and the nurse will measure . . .
3. Next, the nurse will take your . . .
4. Then you'll go to the lab for some blood tests and . . .
5. Next, we'll go into the examination room and I'll look at your . . .

UNIT 1

WORKBOOK PAGE 2

A. What Do They Like to Do?

1. likes to watch TV
2. like to play soccer
3. likes to write letters
4. like to listen to music
5. like to go dancing
6. likes to chat online
7. likes to go hiking
8. like to go to the mall
9. likes to go to the beach

B. Listening

1. b	**3.** a	**5.** a	**7.** b
2. b	**4.** b	**6.** b	**8.** a

WORKBOOK PAGE 3

C. What Do They Like to Do?

1. watch
   He watches
   He watched
   He's going to watch
2. listen
   I listen
   I listened
   I'm going to listen
3. ride
   She rides
   She rode
   She's going to ride
4. sing
   They sing
   They sang
   They're going to sing
5. bake
   We bake
   We baked
   We're going to bake
6. go
   He goes
   He went
   He's going to go

WORKBOOK PAGE 4

D. Likes and Dislikes

1. likes to cook
2. doesn't like to take
3. like to feed
4. don't like to eat
5. likes to read
6. doesn't like to wait
7. like to watch
8. don't like to drive
9. likes to clean
10. don't like to go

WORKBOOK PAGES 5–6

F. Day After Day

1. washes
   He washed
   He's going to wash
2. gets up
   She got up
   She's going to get up
3. go
   They went
   They're going to go
4. study
   I studied
   I'm going to study
5. plays
   He played
   He's going to play
6. makes
   She made
   She's going to make
7. plant
   We planted
   We're going to plant
8. writes
   He wrote
   He's going to write
9. visits
   She visited
   She's going to visit
10. do
    We did
    We're going to do

WORKBOOK PAGE 8

I. What's Paula Going to Give Her Family?

1. She's going to give him gloves.
2. She's going to give her a dog.
3. She's going to give him a watch.
4. She's going to give them a CD player.
5. She's going to give her a sweater.
6. She's going to give him a novel.
7. She's going to give them a plant.
8. She's going to give him a cell phone.

J. Presents

1. gave, I'm going to give him
2. gave, he's going to give her
3. gave, she's going to give him
4. gave, we're going to give them
5. gave, I'm going to give her
6. gave, we're going to give him

WORKBOOK PAGE 9

K. More Presents

1. I, her
2. They, me
3. He, them
4. They, us
5. She, me
6. We, him
7. I, you
8. You, me

WORKBOOK PAGE 10

L. Matching

1. b
2. d
3. a
4. c
5. h
6. f
7. e
8. g

M. What's the Number?

1. 50th
2. 99th
3. 15th
4. 12th
5. 77th
6. 1st
7. 16th
8. 65th
9. 84th
10. 36th

N. Listening

1. 2nd
2. 12th
3. 30th
4. 13th
5. 3rd
6. 9th
7. 1st
8. 19th
9. 17th
10. 4th
11. 48th
12. 5th
13. 34th
14. 26th
15. 62nd
16. 18th

WORKBOOK PAGE 11

O. Richard's Birthdays

1. had
2. made
3. baked
4. gave
5. loved
6. played
7. give
8. went
9. swam
10. went
11. liked
12. like
13. gave
14. wanted
15. had
16. cooked
17. ate
18. played
19. enjoyed
20. talk
21. have
22. went
23. had
24. give
25. cook
26. danced

P. Matching

1. b   2. d   3. a   4. c

UNIT 2

WORKBOOK PAGE 12

A. What's the Food?

1. tomatoes
2. carrots
3. grapes
4. potatoes
5. ice cream
6. apples
7. lettuce
8. bread
9. cake
10. flour
11. onions
12. ketchup
13. mustard
14. eggs
15. meat
16. oranges
17. soy sauce
18. pepper
19. cheese
20. mayonnaise

WORKBOOK PAGE 13

B. What Are They Saying?

1. Where's, It's
2. Where are, They're
3. Where's, It's
4. Where are, They're
5. Where are, They're
6. Where's, It's
7. Where are, They're
8. Where's, It's

C. Listening

1. a
2. b
3. a
4. b
5. a
6. a
7. b
8. a

WORKBOOK PAGE 14

D. I'm Sorry, But . . .

1. there aren't any french fries
2. there isn't any tea
3. there isn't any chicken
4. there aren't any cookies
5. there isn't any cake
6. there aren't any sandwiches
7. there isn't any orange juice
8. there aren't any meatballs

WORKBOOK PAGE 15

E. There Isn't/There Aren't

1. isn't any mayonnaise, mustard
2. aren't any bananas, grapes
3. isn't any meat, fish
4. aren't any apples, pears
5. isn't any ice cream, yogurt
6. aren't any potatoes, rice
7. aren't any tomatoes, onions
8. isn't any milk, orange juice

F. Listening

1. ___ ✔
2. ✔ ___
3. ✔ ___
4. ✔ ___
5. ___ ✔
6. ___ ✔

WORKBOOK PAGE 16

G. What's the Word?

1. How many, too many, a few
2. How much, too much, a little
3. How much, too much, a little
4. How many, too many, a few
5. How much, too much, a little
6. How many, too many, a few

H. What's the Problem?

1. too many   3. too much
2. too much   4. too many

WORKBOOK PAGE 18

J. What's the Word?

1. little, much
2. few, many
3. This, is, it, little
4. These, are, them, few
5. little, it's
6. them, few
7. it's, it
8. many, they're, few

WORKBOOK PAGE 19

K. Matching

1. e   6. g
2. j   7. b
3. h   8. d
4. c   9. f
5. i   10. a

L. Listening

1. ___ ✔
2. ✔ ___
3. ✔ ___
4. ___ ✔
5. ___ ✔
6. ✔ ___
7. ___ ✔
8. ___ ✔
9. ___ ✔
10. ✔ ___

UNIT 3

WORKBOOK PAGE 21

A. Shopping Lists

1. can of, head of, bottle of, pound of, bag of
2. box of, jar of, loaf of, bunch of, dozen
3. gallons of, boxes of, bunches of, pounds of, loaves of

WORKBOOK PAGE 22

B. What Are They Saying?

1. jam
2. ice cream
3. bananas
4. cookies
5. onions
6. cheese

C. Listening

1. ✔ ___ ✔ ___ ✔
2. ___ ✔ ✔ ✔ ___
3. ✔ ___ ___ ✔ ___ ✔
4. ___ ✔ ✔ ___ ✔

WORKBOOK PAGE 24

E. Shopping for Food

1. much, quart, cost
   quart, milk costs
   money
   right, is

2. much, loaf of
   loaf, bread costs
   loaves
   loaves, of
   bread is
3. much does, pound
   pound of, costs
   much
   are
   are

F. Listening

1. $1.99   4. 25¢   7. $3.13
2. $5   5. $2.47   8. $1.50
3. $4.79   6. $6.60   9. $2.10

WORKBOOK PAGE 25

G. What's the Word?

1. b   3. b   5. a
2. a   4. a   6. b

H. Where Would You Like to Go for Lunch?

1. is   13. much
2. it   14. many
3. order   15. piece
4. of   16. of
5. is   17. bowl
6. glass   18. of
7. are   19. dish
8. they   20. of
9. order   21. is
10. of   22. cup
11. are   23. of
12. is

WORKBOOK PAGE 27

K. What's the Word?

1. carrots   5. apples
2. oranges   6. bowl
3. nuts   7. Mix in
4. water   8. Cook

L. What's the Recipe?

1. a little   3. a few, a little   5. a little, a little
2. a few   4. a few   6. a few

M. Listening

1. b   3. a   5. b
2. b   4. a   6. a

WORKBOOK PAGES 28–29

CHECK-UP TEST: Units 1–3

A.

1. bunch   3. bag   5. boxes
2. can   4. piece   6. loaves

B.

1. many
2. much
3. like to
4. much
5. few, them, they're
6. This, is, little

C.

1. drove, He's going to drive
2. went, I'm going to go
3. played, We're going to play
4. wrote, She's going to write
5. made, He's going to make

D.

1. he's going to give her
2. she's going to give him
3. we're going to give them

E.

1. isn't
2. aren't
3. isn't
4. aren't
5. isn't

GAZETTE

WORKBOOK PAGES 29a–b

A. Food Shopping

1. c
2. a
3. b
4. d
5. a
6. c
7. d
8. b

B. Build Your Vocabulary! Crossword

C. Fact File

1. c
2. b
3. c
4. d
5. c
6. b
7. d
8. a

D. "Can-Do" Review

1. e
2. i
3. a
4. h
5. b
6. j
7. d
8. g
9. c
10. f

WORKBOOK PAGE 30

A. Soon

1. I will, I'll be back
2. it will, It'll begin
3. he will, He'll return
4. we will, We'll be ready
5. they will, They'll arrive
6. it will, It'll end
7. she will, She'll be here
8. I will, I'll get out

WORKBOOK PAGE 31

B. We'll Just Have to Wait and See

1. will, she will, she won't
2. will, he will, he won't
3. you'll, will, I won't
4. I'll, will, you won't
5. it'll, it will, it won't
6. there will, there will, there won't
7. will, we will, we won't
8. will, they will, they won't

WORKBOOK PAGE 32

C. What Do You Think?

1. he'll bake, he won't bake
2. she'll order, she won't order
3. they'll go, they won't go
4. I'll get, I won't get
5. it'll arrive, it won't arrive
6. we'll finish, we won't finish

D. Listening

1. want to
2. won't
3. want to
4. won't
5. won't
6. want to
7. won't
8. want to

E. Different Opinions

1. it'll be
2. they'll arrive
3. she'll be
4. he'll buy
5. we'll have

WORKBOOK PAGE 34

G. They Don't Know

1. He might make eggs
   he might make pancakes
2. She might get up at 10 o'clock
   she might get up at noon
3. They might clean it today
   they might clean it tomorrow
4. I might give them a plant
   I might give them a painting
5. We might watch game shows
   we might watch cartoons

6. They might go to Manila
   they might go to Bangkok
7. I might go to the beach
   I might go to a museum
8. He might name it Chester
   he might name it Fluffy

WORKBOOK PAGE 35

H. Be Careful!

1. a   3. a   5. b
2. b   4. a   6. b

I. Loud and Clear

1. Wendy, walk, work, winter, weather
2. waiter, waitress won't walk, wet
3. Walter, wife want, wash, windows, weekend
4. We wanted, water wasn't warm

WORKBOOK PAGES 36–37

J. Pessimists

1. she's afraid she might break her leg
2. he's afraid he might get a sunburn
3. I'm afraid I might drown
4. we're afraid we might miss our bus
5. they're afraid they might get sick
6. he's afraid he might step on her feet
7. we're afraid we might fall asleep
8. I'm afraid I might have a terrible time
9. he's afraid he might get a backache
10. she's afraid she might get seasick
11. I'm afraid I might get fat
12. she's afraid she might catch a cold
13. we're afraid it might rain
14. he's afraid he might look terrible

K. Listening

1. a   6. a
2. b   7. b
3. b   8. b
4. a   9. a
5. b   10. a

WORKBOOK PAGE 39

M. GrammarSong

1. make   7. wide
2. cake   8. decide
3. wide   9. her
4. decide   10. sweater
5. go   11. wide
6. Mexico   12. decide

UNIT 5

WORKBOOK PAGE 40

A. Old and New

1. softer   4. hotter
2. lighter   5. friendlier
3. larger   6. safer

7. smaller   11. easier
8. fancier   12. nicer
9. warmer   13. cheaper
10. bigger   14. uglier

B. What's the Word?

1. shorter   3. fatter
2. cuter   4. busier

WORKBOOK PAGE 41

C. They're Different

1. more talkative
2. more interesting
3. more attractive
4. more comfortable
5. more intelligent
6. longer
7. colder
8. thinner
9. healthier
10. more powerful
11. more handsome
12. whiter
13. more beautiful

D. What's the Word?

1. more delicious   3. more expensive
2. better   4. more energetic

WORKBOOK PAGE 42

E. Puzzle

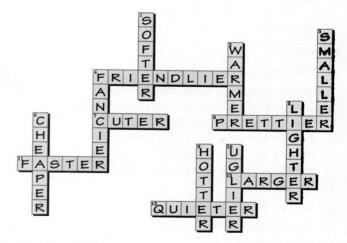

F. Listening

1. a   5. b
2. b   6. a
3. b   7. a
4. a   8. b

WORKBOOK PAGE 43

G. Let's Compare!

1. Jack's tie is fancier than John's tie.
2. The printer is cheaper than the computer.

(continued)

3. The meatballs are more delicious than the chicken.
4. Rick is more talkative than Dick.
5. Carol's car is smaller than Carla's car.
6. Frank is more talented than Fred.

WORKBOOK PAGE 44

I. Listening

1. Yes
2. No
3. No
4. Yes
5. Yes
6. No
7. No
8. Yes

WORKBOOK PAGE 45

K. What Should They Do?

1. You should plant some flowers.
2. He should call the dentist.
3. You should rent a video.
4. You should call the police.
5. They should hire her.
6. She should fire him.

WORKBOOK PAGE 47

N. What's the Word?

1. his
2. mine
3. hers
4. theirs
5. yours
6. his
7. ours

O. What's the Word?

1. yours, mine
2. his, hers
3. ours, theirs
4. Yours, mine
5. hers, his

WORKBOOK PAGE 48

P. Different, But Okay

1. isn't as quiet as, more interesting
2. isn't as fashionable as, more comfortable
3. aren't as modern as, larger
4. isn't as powerful as, more reliable
5. isn't as warm as, sunnier
6. aren't as talkative as, more understanding
7. as exciting as, better

Q. You're Right

1. more attractive than Ken's tie
2. nicer than Donald
3. lazier than Larry
4. more difficult than English
5. bigger than Julie's office
6. more talkative than your son

WORKBOOK PAGE 50

T. Who Should We Hire?

1. lively
2. smarter
3. more talented
4. talented
5. more honest
6. better
7. friendly
8. more intelligent

9. more talkative
10. more polite
11. more capable
12. better
13. delicious
14. more interesting
15. faster
16. nicer

UNIT 6

WORKBOOK PAGE 51

A. What Are They Saying?

1. the brightest
2. the neatest
3. the nicest
4. the fanciest
5. the friendliest
6. the quietest
7. the cutest
8. the biggest
9. the sloppiest
10. the meanest

WORKBOOK PAGE 52

B. What's the Word?

1. talented, the most talented
2. generous, the most generous
3. energetic, the most energetic
4. polite, the most polite
5. smart, the smartest
6. boring, the most boring
7. patient, the most patient
8. honest, the most honest
9. noisy, the noisiest
10. interesting, the most interesting
11. stubborn, the most stubborn

WORKBOOK PAGE 53

C. Worldbuy.com

1. the most attractive
2. the softest
3. the most elegant
4. the most modern
5. the warmest
6. the best
7. the most reliable
8. the most beautiful
9. the most delicious

WORKBOOK PAGE 55

E. The Best in the World!

1. more powerful, the most powerful
2. more lightweight, the most lightweight
3. more efficient, the most efficient
4. more dependable, the most dependable
5. brighter, the brightest

WORKBOOK PAGE 56

F. Listening

1. more comfortable
2. the worst

3. more energetic
4. cheaper
5. the most important
6. the sloppiest
7. the best
8. lazy
9. meaner
10. the most honest

G. Puzzle

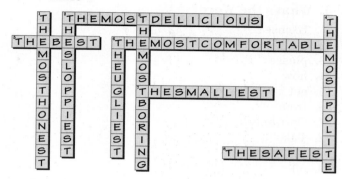

WORKBOOK PAGE 57

H. Loud and Clear

1. Andrew, worst actor, terrible, program
2. recommend Carla's recipe, fruitcake, better
3. Robert, friendlier, more energetic, brother
4. Rita reads, newspaper, morning, writes
5. Ronald, sister, perfume, thirtieth birthday
6. car, bigger, more powerful, neighbor's

WORKBOOK PAGES 58–59

CHECK-UP TEST: Units 4–6

A.
1. it will, It'll
2. they won't
3. I will, I'll
4. she won't
5. we will, We'll

B.
1. might
2. Should
3. might, might
4. should

C.
1. mine
2. his
3. theirs
4. yours

D.
1. taller than
2. more honest than
3. prettier than
4. better than
5. more dependable than

E.
1. isn't as fast as, more reliable
2. isn't as friendly as, cuter
3. isn't as intelligent as, more interesting
4. isn't as fashionable as, bigger
5. isn't as expensive as, more attractive

F.
1. the quietest
2. the most hospitable
3. the largest
4. the most patient
5. the laziest

G.
1. Yes
2. No
3. No
4. Yes
5. No

GAZETTE

WORKBOOK PAGES 59a–d

A. Did You Know?
1. d
2. b
3. a
4. c
5. d
6. b

D. Build Your Vocabulary! Prefixes
1. im
2. un
3. un
4. in
5. un
6. dis
7. un
8. im

E. Build Your Vocabulary! What's the Word?
1. inexpensive
2. unsafe
3. dishonest
4. unhealthy
5. uncomfortable
6. impatient
7. impolite
8. unfriendly

F. Build Your Vocabulary! Prefix or No Prefix?
1. healthy
2. impolite
3. uncomfortable
4. honest
5. expensive
6. impatient
7. friendly
8. unsafe

G. Build Your Vocabulary! What's the Prefix?
1. unkind
2. unfashionable
3. unreliable
4. inconvenient
5. uninteresting
6. inhospitable

H. Fact File
1. d
2. c
3. b
4. b
5. d
6. a
7. b
8. d
9. c
10. b

I. "Can-Do" Review
1. c
2. i
3. a
4. f
5. b
6. d
7. h
8. j
9. g
10. e

UNIT 7

WORKBOOK PAGE 60

A. How Do I Get There?
1. Walk up, on the right, across from
2. Walk up, on the left, next to
3. Walk up, on the right, across from

(continued)

4. Walk down, on the left, between
5. Walk down, on the right, next to, across from

WORKBOOK PAGE 61

B. Which Way?

1. Walk along, on the right, across from
2. Walk along, on the left, next to
3. Walk up, on the right, across from
4. Walk down, on the left, next to
5. Walk along, on the right, between

WORKBOOK PAGES 62–63

C. Let's Help Mr. and Mrs. Lee!

1. Walk along
turn left
Walk up
on the right
across from
2. Walk up
turn left
Walk along
on the left
between
3. Walk along
turn left
Walk down
on the right
next to
4. Walk down
turn right
Walk along
on the left
across from

D. Listening

1. a	**3.** a	**5.** b
2. b	**4.** b	**6.** a

WORKBOOK PAGE 65

F. In a Hurry!

1. Take
get off
Center Street
Walk up
Center
on the right
2. Take
get off
River Street
Walk down
River
on the left
3. Take
get off
State Street
Walk up
State
on the right

WORKBOOK PAGE 67

I. Listening: *Where Did They Go?*

1. bank
2. library
3. bakery
4. museum
5. zoo
6. park

J. What's the Word?

1. Excuse
2. Could
3. please
4. how
5. get
6. from
7. Certainly
8. Take
9. subway
10. off
11. up
12. turn
13. Walk
14. left
15. between

UNIT 8

WORKBOOK PAGE 68

A. What Do You Think?

1. terribly
2. accurately
3. gracefully
4. badly
5. carefully
6. dishonestly
7. carelessly
8. slowly
9. fast
10. beautiful
11. hard
12. good

WORKBOOK PAGE 69

B. Answer

Careful
Carefully

1. careful, carefully
2. terribly, good
3. beautifully, graceful
4. good, fast
5. safely, careless
6. badly, politely
7. cheaply, expensive
8. reliable, energetically

C. Listening

1. slow
2. beautifully
3. dishonest
4. sloppily
5. accurate
6. rudely
7. safely
8. reliable
9. softly
10. cheaply
11. carefully
12. patient

WORKBOOK PAGE 71

E. What's the Word?

1. faster
2. louder/more loudly
3. more carefully
4. more accurately
5. quicker/more quickly
6. more gracefully
7. better
8. harder
9. slower/more slowly

WORKBOOK PAGE 72

F. Ralph Should Try Harder!

1. earlier
2. neater/more neatly
3. slower/more slowly
4. more politely
5. faster/quicker/more quickly
6. more carefully
7. softer/more softly

WORKBOOK PAGE 73

H. GrammarSong

1. careful
2. carefully
3. careful
4. carefully
5. beautiful
6. beautifully
7. beautiful
8. beautifully
9. graceful
10. gracefully
11. graceful
12. gracefully
13. stronger
14. longer
15. better
16. better

WORKBOOK PAGE 74

I. What's the Answer?

1. a
2. b
3. a
4. b
5. b
6. a
7. a
8. b
9. a
10. a
11. b
12. b

J. Matching

1. d
2. f
3. a
4. c
5. b
6. e

WORKBOOK PAGE 75

K. If

1. arrive, we'll
2. it rains
3. is, will go
4. plays, he'll have
5. make, will be
6. touches, he'll get
7. it's, will go
8. eats, she'll get
9. do, I'll be
10. have, we'll name
11. there's, will
12. go, they'll eat/they'll have

L. Scrambled Sentences

1. If he goes to the party, he'll wear his new suit.
2. If she misses the bus, she'll be late for work.
3. If I practice, I'll play chess better.
4. If I go to the bakery, I'll buy an apple pie.
5. If you don't finish school, you'll be sorry.
6. If Sam works hard in school, he'll get a good job.

WORKBOOK PAGE 78

P. Please Don't!

1. I have to read
2. I'll
3. I'm
4. I fall asleep
5. won't
6. he'll/she'll
7. they're
8. they tell
9. he'll/she'll
10. he'll
11. he's
12. he'll
13. he has
14. won't
15. he doesn't
16. he'll be
17. he's
18. he'll

WORKBOOK PAGES 79–80

CHECK-UP TEST: Units 7–8

A.

1. terribly
2. carefully
3. badly
4. hard

B.

1. honest, dishonestly
2. quick, quiet
3. good, well
4. safely, careless

C.

1. later
2. more politely
3. more gracefully
4. louder/more loudly

D.

1. eat/have, you'll
2. is, will be
3. have, they'll name
4. I'm not

E.

1. we take, we'll go
2. feel, might go
3. might get
4. doesn't, I'll go

F.

1. ice cream shop
2. concert hall
3. shopping mall
4. hotel
5. book store

GAZETTE

WORKBOOK PAGES 80a–b

A. You're Hired!

1. b	**3.** d	**5.** a	**7.** b
2. c	**4.** c	**6.** d	**8.** c

B. Build Your Vocabulary! What's the Job?

1. gardener	**4.** supervisor
2. programmer	**5.** director
3. photographer	**6.** designer

C. Build Your Vocabulary! Crossword

D. "Can-Do" Review

1. f	**5.** c	**8.** d
2. h	**6.** i	**9.** b
3. a	**7.** e	**10.** g
4. j		

UNIT 9

WORKBOOK PAGE 81

A. What Were They Doing?

1. He was driving to the beach.
2. She was walking down Main Street.
3. They were jogging.
4. We were playing basketball.
5. He was riding his motorcycle.
6. She was fixing her fence.

7. They were painting their house.
8. We were skateboarding.

WORKBOOK PAGE 82

B. What Were They Doing?

1. were baking
2. was wearing
3. were playing
4. was riding
5. were watching
6. was sleeping
7. were having
8. was chatting
9. was talking

WORKBOOK PAGE 83

D. The Wrong Day!

1. He was cleaning
2. She was vacuuming
3. He was sweeping
4. She was washing
5. They were making
6. They were baking

E. Listening

1. a		**5.** b
2. b		**6.** a
3. b		**7.** a
4. a		**8.** b

WORKBOOK PAGE 84

F. What's the Word?

1. into	**5.** on
2. out of	**6.** along
3. off	**7.** out of
4. into	**8.** off

G. Listening

5 2 6 3

8 4 1 7

WORKBOOK PAGE 86

I. Nobody Wants To

1. myself
2. herself
3. ourselves
4. yourself
5. themselves
6. himself
7. yourselves

J. What's the Word?

1. a
2. b
3. b
4. a
5. a
6. b

WORKBOOK PAGE 87

K. What Happened?

1. tripped, she was walking
2. bit, he was riding
3. fainted, he was watching
4. stole, we were having
5. dropped, she was getting on
6. cut, I was shaving
7. burned, they were cooking
8. lost, he was roller-blading
9. hurt, we were skiing
10. fell, they were painting

WORKBOOK PAGE 88

L. What's the Word?

1. up
2. over
3. on
4. out of
5. at
6. through
7. under

M. Listening

1. a
2. b
3. b
4. a
5. a
6. b
7. b
8. a
9. b
10. a
11. a
12. b

WORKBOOK PAGE 90

O. Loud and Clear

1. niece, reading, e-mail, keypal, Greece
2. William tripped, himself, his office building
3. Steve, asleep, three fifteen, cookies, cheese
4. Hill, busy, clinic, children, city, sick
5. Lee, beach, Tahiti, sleeping, she's, CDs
6. little sister, isn't, sandwich, spilled, milk

UNIT 10

WORKBOOK PAGE 91

A. What's the Word?

1. couldn't, can
2. couldn't, can
3. couldn't, can
4. couldn't
5. can't
6. could, could
7. couldn't

8. couldn't, can
9. couldn't
10. couldn't, could
11. can't
12. couldn't

WORKBOOK PAGE 94

D. What's the Word?

1. couldn't/wasn't able to, had to
2. couldn't/wasn't able to, had to
3. could/was able to
4. couldn't/wasn't able to
5. could/were able to, couldn't/wasn't able to, had to
6. couldn't/weren't able to, had to
7. could/was able to, could/was able to, couldn't/wasn't able to, couldn't/ wasn't able to
8. couldn't/weren't able to, had to
9. couldn't/wasn't able to, had to

WORKBOOK PAGE 95

F. What's the Word?

1. b
2. b
3. a
4. b
5. b
6. a

WORKBOOK PAGE 96

G. Why Not?

1. He's got to
2. She's got to
3. I've got to
4. We've got to
5. He's got to
6. They've got to
7. you've got to

WORKBOOK PAGE 97

H. My Friend Lisa

1. She won't be able to go jogging every morning.
2. She won't be able to ride her bicycle to school every day.
3. She won't be able to play tennis on the school team.
4. She won't be able to swim every afternoon.
5. She won't be able to do exercises every evening.
6. She'll be able to play the violin.
7. She'll be able to bake delicious cakes and cookies.
8. She'll be able to make her own clothes.
9. She'll be able to fix her computer when it's broken.

I. They'll Be Able To

1. couldn't, she'll be able to
2. couldn't, we'll be able to
3. couldn't, he'll be able to
4. couldn't, I'll be able to

J. They Won't Be Able To

1. won't be able to, I've got to
2. won't be able to, She's got to
3. won't be able to, they've got to
4. won't be able to, he's got to
5. won't be able to, We've got to

K. Listening

1. b   3. a   5. a
2. a   4. b   6. b

WORKBOOK PAGE 100

N. GrammarSong

1. day   8. day
2. today   9. day
3. go   10. today
4. no   11. go
5. to   12. no
6. do   13. to
7. play   14. do

WORKBOOK PAGES 101–102

CHECK-UP TEST: Units 9–10

A.

1. were playing   5. were reading
2. was driving   6. was riding
3. were jogging   7. was sitting
4. was shaving

B.

1. ourselves   4. yourself
2. himself   5. themselves
3. yourselves   6. herself

C.

1. off   5. into
2. on   6. couldn't
3. out of   7. won't be able to
4. through   8. couldn't, had to

D.

1. wasn't   5. wasn't, had to
2. will be   6. you've
3. weren't   7. won't be, she's
4. I'll be

E.

1. b   2. a   3. b   4. b

GAZETTE

WORKBOOK PAGES 102a–c

A. Families and Time

1. c   3. c   5. a   7. d
2. d   4. b   6. b   8. c

C. Build Your Vocabulary! Mixed-Up Words

1. dryer   5. microwave
2. toaster   6. garbage disposal
3. iron   7. coffee maker
4. dishwasher   8. washing machine

D. Build Your Vocabulary! Categories

Appliances for Clothing Care
dryer   iron   washing machine

Appliances for Food Preparation
toaster   microwave   coffee maker

Appliances for Food Cleanup
dishwasher   garbage disposal

E. Build Your Vocabulary! What's the Word?

1. dryer   5. washing machine
2. garbage disposal 6. iron
3. microwave   7. toaster
4. dishwasher   8. coffee maker

F. Fact File

1. b   3. b   5. a   7. c
2. d   4. c   6. d   8. b

G. "Can-Do" Review

1. g   5. a   8. j
2. d   6. b   9. c
3. h   7. e   10. f
4. i

UNIT 11

WORKBOOK PAGE 103

A. Matching

1. d   5. a
2. g   6. b
3. e   7. f
4. h   8. c

B. How Was Your Medical Checkup?

1. b   6. a
2. b   7. b
3. a   8. b
4. b   9. a
5. a   10. b

WORKBOOK PAGE 104

C. Wendy Is Worried About Her Health

1. fewer   9. less
2. less   10. fewer
3. more   11. more
4. more   12. more
5. fewer   13. fewer
6. less   14. less
7. more   15. more
8. more   16. more

WORKBOOK PAGE 106

E. First Day at a New Job

1. must dress, must type
2. must answer, must repair
3. must arrive, must work
4. must sort, must file
5. must dance, must sing
6. must cook, must speak

WORKBOOK PAGE 107

F. What's the Word?

1. mustn't
2. mustn't
3. don't have to, mustn't
4. don't have to
5. don't have to, mustn't
6. mustn't
7. doesn't have to

G. The Butler School

1. must
2. must
3. must
4. don't have to
5. must
6. don't have to
7. must
8. mustn't
9. must
10. mustn't
11. mustn't
12. must
13. don't have to
14. must

WORKBOOK PAGE 109

J. Listening

1. b
2. a
3. a
4. b
5. b
6. a

WORKBOOK PAGE 110

M. Loud and Clear

1. Hi, happy, here, hotel, Honolulu Hawaii
2. Howard, have, hand, history homework, half
3. Harry, hurt his head, have, helmet
4. Henry, heavy, height, has, having hot dogs
5. Hilda's husband, healthy, He has, heart
6. Hillary, happy, has, hiccups, horrible headache

UNIT 12

WORKBOOK PAGE 111

A. They'll All Be Busy

1. Yes, he will. He'll be mopping
2. Yes, they will. They'll be bathing
3. Yes, we will. We'll be exercising
4. Yes, they will. They'll be paying
5. Yes, she will. She'll be knitting
6. Yes, I will. I'll be sewing
7. Yes, he will. He'll be ironing
8. Yes, we will. We'll be rearranging

WORKBOOK PAGES 114–115

D. Why Don't You?

1. she'll be practicing the violin
   practices the violin
2. he'll be studying
   studies
3. they'll be doing their laundry
   do their laundry
4. she'll be exercising
   exercises
5. he'll be cleaning his apartment
   cleans his apartment
6. they'll be watching TV
   watch TV
7. she'll be washing her car
   washes her car
8. they'll be baking
   bake
9. he'll be taking a bath
   takes a bath
10. they'll be bathing their dog
    bathe their dog

E. Listening

1. b
2. a
3. b
4. a
5. a
6. b
7. b
8. a
9. b
10. a
11. b
12. b

WORKBOOK PAGE 116

F. What's the Word?

1. Hello
2. This
3. May
4. speak
5. isn't
6. right
7. take
8. message
9. tell
10. that
11. called
12. Okay

G. What's the Response?

1. b
2. a
3. b
4. a
5. b
6. a
7. b
8. b
9. b
10. a
11. b
12. a

WORKBOOK PAGE 117

H. Until When?

1. I'll be practicing, for
2. He'll be reading, until
3. She'll be working, until
4. We'll be arriving, at
5. I'll be having, in
6. She'll be studying, until
7. He'll be staying, until
8. I'll be cooking, for

I. What's the Question?

1. will you be talking on the telephone
2. will they be arriving
3. will she be working on his car
4. will he be leaving
5. will we be driving
6. will you be mopping the floors
7. will she be feeding the dog
8. will they be living away from home
9. will he be playing loud music
10. will we be riding on the roller-coaster

UNIT 13

WORKBOOK PAGE 120

A. By Themselves

1. His, him, himself
2. Their, them, themselves
3. Her, her, herself
4. you, You, yourself
5. him, himself
6. myself, me
7. Our, us, ourselves
8. yourselves, you

WORKBOOK PAGE 121

B. The Lost Rollerblades

1. yours
2. mine
3. his
4. hers
5. theirs
6. ours

C. Scrambled Sentences

1. Did he fix his car by himself?
2. Is this address book yours?
3. She can feed the cats by herself.
4. Did you give him her telephone number?
5. When you call Bob, tell him I have his new sunglasses.
6. I need to use your cell phone because I lost mine.

WORKBOOK PAGE 122

D. What's the Word?

1. a
2. b
3. b
4. b
5. a
6. b
7. a
8. b

E. Listening

1. b
2. b
3. a
4. a
5. c
6. c

F. Noisy Neighbors

1. neighbors'
2. are listening
3. listened
4. for
5. wasn't
6. fall
7. hard
8. at
9. he'll call
10. his
11. next-door
12. their
13. noisy
14. to complain
15. move
16. to
17. myself
18. her
19. are barking
20. loudly
21. barked
22. until
23. might
24. to argue
25. nice
26. to be tired
27. I'm practicing
28. during
29. until
30. I eat
31. a few
32. tells
33. have to
34. don't
35. won't
36. well

WORKBOOK PAGES 125–126

G. What's the Word?

1. anything
   nobody
   anything
   anybody
2. anything
   nobody
   yourself
3. Somebody
   Nobody
4. someone
   any
5. anybody
   someone
6. anyone
   nobody

7. somebody
anything
Nobody
something
Nobody

H. Listening: *The Prom*

1. b
2. a
3. b
4. a
5. b
6. b

WORKBOOK PAGE 129

L. Listening

1. b
2. c
3. b
4. c
5. a
6. b
7. c
8. b

WORKBOOK PAGE 130

M. What's the **Word?**

1. Two, too
2. week, weak
3. They're, their
4. right, write
5. Where, wear
6. hour, our
7. know, No
8. buy, by
9. hole, whole
10. You're, Your
11. eight, ate

WORKBOOK PAGES 132–133

CHECK-UP TEST: Units 11–13

A.

1. They'll be paying
2. I'll be going
3. He'll be reading
4. She'll be working
5. We'll be getting married

B.

1. will you be practicing the piano
2. will he be ironing
3. will she be leaving
4. will they be driving
5. will you be chatting online

C.

1. less, fewer, less
2. don't have to
3. mustn't, much
4. don't have to
5. for
6. until
7. at
8. at
9. someone, anything
10. somebody
11. Someone
12. mine
13. their, hers
14. her
15. ours

D.

1. a	**4.** b
2. b	**5.** a
3. a	

GAZETTE

WORKBOOK PAGES 133a–c

A. Communities

1. c	**3.** c	**5.** d	**7.** a
2. d	**4.** b	**6.** b	**8.** c

C. Build Your Vocabulary! What's the Word?

1. a chimneysweep
2. TV repairperson
3. an exterminator
4. an installer
5. appliance repairperson

D. Build Your Vocabulary! Crossword

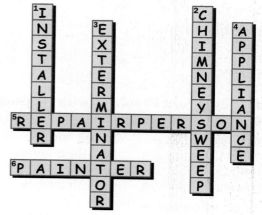

E. Fact File

1. d	**3.** c	**5.** c	**7.** b
2. b	**4.** b	**6.** a	**8.** c

F. "Can-Do" Review

1. i	**5.** j	**8.** d
2. e	**6.** c	**9.** b
3. g	**7.** h	**10.** f
4. a		

ACTIVITY WORKBOOK 2 ANSWER KEY: Pages 135–164

UNIT 1: Workbook Pages 135–136

A. Days, Months, and Abbreviations

1. Wednesday
2. Monday
3. Saturday
4. Tuesday
5. Friday
6. Thursday
7. Sunday
8. March
9. October
10. January
11. May
12. November
13. February
14. July
15. August
16. December
17. June
18. April
19. September

B. Dates

1. 01/08/17
2. 07/10/18
3. 03/12/16
4. 05/03/14
5. 09/05/15
6. 11/30/20
7. 04/09/19
8. 02/22/17
9. 08/01/89
10. 10/02/16
11. 12/06/18
12. 06/04/05

D. Numeracy: A Calendar, Dates, and Ordinal Numbers

1. Monday, November <u>7</u>
2. Tuesday, November <u>8</u>
3. Thursday November <u>17</u>
4. Wednesday, November <u>30</u>
5. 11/10/1996
6. 11/14/1976
7. 11/23/2004
8. 11/18/1968
9. 11/20/1991
10. 11/05/1966

E. The American School System

<u>6</u> <u>3</u> <u>1</u>
<u>2</u> <u>4</u> <u>5</u>

UNIT 2: Workbook Pages 137–138

A. School Personnel

1. g
2. e
3. f
4. d
5. a
6. c
7. b

B. A School Floor Plan

1. T
2. F
3. F
4. T
5. T
6. T
7. F
8. T
9. T
10. F

C. Numeracy: Word Problems with Elapsed Time

1. <u>30</u> minutes
2. <u>6</u> hours
3. <u>3</u> hours
4. <u>3</u> hours and <u>45</u> minutes
5. <u>3</u> hours
6. <u>45</u> minutes
7. <u>2</u> hours and <u>15</u> minutes

D. Parts of a Computer

1. keyboard
2. monitor
3. mouse
4. power cable
5. power button
6. USB port

UNIT 3: Workbook Pages 139–141

A. A Supermarket Receipt

1. $2.99
2. $1.99
3. $4.50
4. $ .25
5. $3.00
6. gallon, quart
7. $24.94

B. A Food Label

1. a
2. b
3. b
4. c
5. b
6. a

C. Numeracy: Supermarket Math – Receipts

1. $14.50
2. $5.50
3. $3.88
4. $10.25

D. Numeracy: Supermarket Math – Unit Pricing

1. Ray's
2. Green's
3. Ray's
4. Green's
5. Green's
6. Ray's

E. Units of Measure & Their Abbreviations

1. fluid ounce
2. teaspoon
3. cup
4. tablespoon
5. gallon
6. quart
7. pint
8. pound

F. Numeracy: Units of Measure

<u>4</u>
<u>2</u>
<u>3</u>
<u>7</u>
<u>5</u>
<u>1</u>
<u>6</u>

G. Numeracy: Quantities in a Recipe

gallon   gallon   pint   quart   pound

UNIT 4: Workbook Page 142

A. An Invitation

1. F
2. F
3. F
4. T
5. T
6. F
7. F
8. T

B. Numeracy: Word Problems with Elapsed Time

1. b
2. c
3. c
4. b

UNIT 5: Workbook Pages 143–144

A. Reading an Advertisement

1. T
2. T
3. F
4. T
5. T
6. F
7. T

C. Numeracy: Using Math to Compare Products

1. c
2. b
3. a
4. d
5. a
6. d

D. Numeracy: Word Problems with Comparatives

1. b
2. a
3. b
4. c

UNIT 6: Workbook Pages 145–147

A. Clothing Labels

1. T	6. T	11. T	16. F
2. T	7. T	12. T	17. F
3. F	8. F	13. F	18. F
4. F	9. T	14. F	19. F
5. T	10. T	15. F	20. T

B. Using an ATM

1. a	3. b	5. c
2. c	4. b	6. b

C. Parts of a Check

1. Mei Ling
2. Southern Gas Company
3. August 2, 2018
4. $76.04

D. Writing Checks

(*Students should enter current date and sign the checks.*)

Community Telephone Company $45.10
Forty-five and 10/100

Gray's Department Store $76.50
Seventy-six and 50/100

E. Numeracy: Balancing a Checkbook

Number	Date	Transaction	Debit	Credit	Balance
150	4/21	Transworld Credit Card	850.50		753.50
	4/23	Paycheck		1,245.00	1,998.50
151	4/28	Milton Electric Company	53.50		1,945.00
152	4/28	Star Gas Company	45.00		1,900.00
153	5/1	Benson Realty	750.00		1,150.00
154	5/6	CCS Cable Company	110.00		1,040.00
	5/7	Paycheck		1,245.00	2,285.00
155	5/9	United Phone Services	84.50		2,200.50

UNIT 7: Workbook Pages 148–149

A. Business Schedules

1. 10:00
2. 12:00
3. Monday, Sunday
4. 9
5. Monday, Tuesday
6. barber shop
7. museum
8. shopping mall

B. A Train Schedule

1. F	4. T	7. T	9. F
2. F	5. F	8. T	10. F
3. T	6. F		

C. Numeracy: Weights & Measurements for Using Postal Services

1. b	5. $2.32	8. First Class
2. a	6. $1.99	9. Express
3. $0.75	7. Express	10. Priority
4. $1.14		

UNIT 8: Workbook Pages 150–152

A. Help Wanted Ad Abbreviations

1. hour	5. Monday to Friday	9. experience
2. week	6. evenings	10. excellent
3. month	7. required	11. full-time
4. years	8. preferred	12. part-time

B. Reading Help Wanted Ads

1. c	2. b	3. d	4. a

D. Numeracy: A Paycheck and a Pay Stub

1. 45 hours	4. $75.00	7. $550.00
2. $65.00	5. $3,035.00	8. 1,620 hours
3. $2,665.00	6. $350.00	9. $420.00

E. Reading an Accident Report

1. F	2. F	3. T	4. F	5. T

UNIT 9: Workbook Pages 153–154

A. Emergencies at Home

1. emergency numbers
2. first-aid kit
3. fire extinguisher
4. smoke detectors
5. utilities
6. dial 911

B. First-Aid

1. e	3. f	5. d
2. c	4. a	6. b

C. A First-Aid Kit

1. j	3. g	5. d	7. b	9. h
2. f	4. c	6. a	8. i	10. e

D. Numeracy: Reading Statistical Information in Tables

1. F	7. Louisiana
2. T	8. Georgia, Maine, Rhode Island
3. F	9. Virginia
4. T	10. Florida
5. T	11. 23
6. F	12. 14

UNIT 10: Workbook Pages 155–156

A. Inquiring about an Apartment for Rent

1. available
2. rent
3. utilities
4. deposit
5. allowed
6. parking
7. transportation

B. Housing Repairs

1. bathtub, sink, toilet
2. bathtub, dishwasher, sink, toilet
3. dishwasher, light, stove

C. Apartment Ads

1. A
2. C
3. A
4. B
5. A
6. B
7. C
8. B
9. A
10. B
11. C
12. A
13. B
14. A

D. Numeracy: Square Footage in a Housing Floor Plan

1. c
2. a
3. b
4. c
5. c
6. b

E. Apartment Building Rules and Regulations

1. N
2. N
3. Y
4. Y
5. N
6. Y
7. N
8. Y
9. Y
10. N
11. N
12. N
13. N
14. Y
15. N

UNIT 11: Workbook Pages 157–159

A. Parts of the Face

1. forehead
2. eye
3. cheek
4. jaw
5. tongue
6. eyebrow
7. nose
8. lip
9. teeth
10. chin

B. Parts of the Body

1. neck
2. throat
3. arm
4. elbow
5. wrist
6. finger
7. ankle
8. toes
9. head
10. shoulder
11. chest
12. hip
13. hand
14. knee
15. foot

C. Reading Medicine Labels

1. 2 capsules every six hours
2. It may upset your stomach.
3. 08/20
4. one tablet every four hours
5. 16
6. 03/19
7. 6 tablets
8. 2 pills every six hours
9. It may make you drowsy.

D. Nutrition: Categorizing Nutrients and Food

Protein: beans, fish
Dairy: low-fat milk, low-fat yogurt
Grains: cereal, rice
Sugar: desserts, soda
Bad Fats: fried foods, mayonnaise
Minerals: calcium, potassium

E. Numeracy: Units of Measure

1. c
2. b
3. a
4. c

F. Numeracy: Adjusting a Recipe

1.

1	egg
1	cup milk
½	teaspoon salt
1½	cups flour
1½	teaspoons baking powder
1	tablespoon oil

2.

4	eggs
2	pints milk
2	teaspoons salt
6	cups flour
2	tablespoons baking powder
¼	cup oil

UNIT 12: Workbooks Page 160–162

A. A Telephone Directory

1. c
2. d
3. b
4. a
5. c
6. d

B. The Yellow Pages

1. T
2. F
3. T
4. F
5. T
6. F
7. F
8. F

C. A Telephone Bil

1. a
2. c
3. c
4. b
5. c
6. a
7. b

D. Numeracy: Fahrenheit & Celsius Tempartures

1. c
2. b
3. f
4. e
5. d
6. g
7. a

E. Numeracy: Word Problems with Elapsed Time

1. c
2. a
3. b
4. c
5. a
6. b

UNIT 13: Workbook Pages 163–164

A. A Rental Agreement

1. T
2. F
3. T
4. T
5. F
6. T

B. Tenants' Rights and Responsibilities

1. L
2. L
3. T
4. L
5. T
6. L

C. Numeracy: Word Problems about Rent with Multiple Operations

1. b
2. b
3. c
4. a
5. c
6. b
7. b
8. a

Correlation Key

STUDENT BOOK PAGES	ACTIVITY WORKBOOK PAGES
Chapter 1	
2	2
3	3
4–5	4–7
6	8
7	9–11
10a	135
10b–d	136
Chapter 2	
12	12–13
13	14–15
14	16–17
15	18–20
18a–b	137–138 Exercise C
18c	138 Exercise D
Chapter 3	
20	21–23
21	24
23	25–26
24	27
26a–d	139–141
Check–Up Test	28–29
Gazette	29a–b
Chapter 4	
30	30
31	31–33
33	34
34	35
35	36–39
38a–d	142
Chapter 5	
40	40
41	41–42
42–43	43–46
45	47–49
47	50
48a–b	143–144
Chapter 6	
50	51
51	52–54
54–55	55–57
58a	145
58b	146–147
Check–Up Test	58–59
Gazette	59a–d
Chapter 7	
62	60
63	61
64–65	62–64
66	65–66
67	67
70a–b	148–149

STUDENT BOOK PAGES	ACTIVITY WORKBOOK PAGES
Chapter 8	
72	68–70
73	71
74	72–73
76	74–76
77	77
79	78
80a–c	150
80d	151
80e	152
Check–Up Test	79–80
Gazette	80a–b
Chapter 9	
84	81–83
85	84–85
87	86
88–89	87–90
92a	153 Exercise A
92b	153 Exercises B–C
92c	154
Chapter 10	
94	91–92
95	93
96	94–95
98–99	96–97
101	98–100
102a	155 Exercises A–B
102b	155 Exercise C, 156 Exercise D
102c	156 Exercise E
Check–Up Test	101–102
Gazette	102a–c
Chapter 11	
106–107	103
108–109	104–106
111	107–108
112	109
113	110
114a	157
114b	158 Exercise C
114c	158 Exercise D, 159
Chapter 12	
116	111
117	112–113
119	114–115
120	116
122	117–119
124a–b	160 Exercise A
124c–d	160 Exercise B, 161–162
Chapter 13	
126	120
127	121
128–129	122–124
130	125
131–132	126–130
136a–d	163–164
Check–Up Test	131–132
Gazette	133a–c

SIDE by SIDE *Plus* Activity Workbook Audio Program

The *Side by Side Plus* Activity Workbook Digital Audio CDs contain all listening activities and GrammarRaps and GrammarSongs for entertaining language practice through rhythm and music. Students can use the Audio Program to extend their language learning through self-study outside the classroom. The Digital Audio CDs also include MP3 files of the audio program for downloading to a computer or audio player.

Audio Program Contents